Essential Histories

The Northern Ireland Troubles

Operation *Banner* 1969–2007

Essential Histories

The Northern Ireland Troubles

Operation *Banner* 1969–2007

Aaron Edwards

First published in Great Britain in 2011 by Osprey Publishing,
Midland House, West Way, Botley, Oxford, OX2 0PH, UK
44-02 23rd Street, Suite 219, Long Island City, NY 11101, USA
E-mail: info@ospreypublishing.com

Osprey Publishing is part of the Osprey Group

A CIP catalogue record for this book is available from the
British Library

Print ISBN: 978 1 84908 525 0
PDF ebook ISBN: 978 1 84908 852 7

Page layout by The Black Spot
Index by Alison Worthington
Typeset in GillSans and ITC Stone Serif
Maps by Peter Bull
Originated by Blenheim Colour, UK
Printed in China through Bookbuilders

11 12 13 14 15   10 9 8 7 6 5 4 3 2 1

Author's note

Protestant Unionists who wish to maintain the Union between
Great Britain and Northern Ireland use the terms 'Northern
Ireland' and 'the province'. Irish nationalists who aspire to a
United Ireland use the terms 'the North' and 'the six counties'.
After the Irish Republican Army split in 1969–70, those who
remained with the leadership became known as the Official IRA;
those who left formed the Provisional IRA (PIRA).

Dedication

For my father, James Edwards – *veritas numquam perit*

Acknowledgements

I would like to thank my interviewees, as well as Tim Bean, James
Edwards, Ed Flint, Gregory Fremont-Barnes, Thomas Hennessey,
Chris Johnson, Malachi O'Doherty, and my partner Jennifer for all
their help and support.

Special mention should be made of two invaluable resources for
the history of Ireland in the period covered by this book – the
website www.irelandstory.com and the CAIN web service.

Editor's note

The opinions expressed here are the author's and not necessarily
those of the Royal Military Academy Sandhurst, the Ministry of
Defence or any other UK Government agency.

Imperial War Museum Collections

Many of the photos in this book come from the Imperial War
Museum's huge collections which cover all aspects of conflict
involving Britain and the Commonwealth since the start of the
twentieth century. These rich resources are available online to
search, browse and buy at www.iwmcollections.org.uk. In addition
to Collections Online, you can visit the Visitor Rooms where you
can explore over 8 million photographs, thousands of hours of
moving images, the largest sound archive of its kind in the world,
thousands of diaries and letters written by people in wartime,
and a huge reference library. To make an appointment, call (020)
7416 5320, or e-mail mail@iwm.org.uk.

Osprey Publishing is supporting the Woodland Trust, the UK's
leading woodland conservation charity, by funding the dedication
of trees.

www.ospreypublishing.com

Contents

Introduction

For more than a generation Northern Ireland was the site of one of Europe's most bloody and protracted recent conflicts. Between 1969 and 2007 the Troubles, as the conflict became euphemistically known, claimed the lives of around 3,700 people, with over ten times as many injured in countless bomb and gun attacks. The sectarian nature of the conflict, together with the indiscriminate character of the violence, entrenched the bitterness and hatred that continues to polarize relations between and within communities in Northern Ireland today. But what are the origins of the Troubles? How did the main protagonists fight their 'war'? And why did political violence persist for so long? Moreover, what lessons can be drawn from the transition from the long war to – hopefully – a long peace?

Although the conflict between Protestant Unionists and Catholic Nationalists has its roots in the settler–native confrontations of the 17th century, its most recent phase can be traced to the partition of Ireland and the formation of a separate Northern Ireland in the 1920s, and the subsequent hold over politics, culture and society enjoyed by the Ulster Unionist Party until the collapse of the Stormont administration in 1972. In the late 1960s a conglomerate of Catholics, nationalists, Republicans and agnostic socialists – along with a handful of Protestants – opposed to Unionist dominance founded the Northern Ireland Civil Rights Association (NICRA). The organization aimed 'to bring to Northern Ireland effective democracy, and to end all the forms of injustice, intimidation, discrimination and deprivation, which result from the partisan rule of the Stormont regime'. Many activists were exercised by what they saw as the local Unionist regime's discriminatory policies towards them in jobs, housing and electoral politics, while a minority of extremists were intent on sparking civil unrest and anarchy. The storm whipped up by NICRA protest marches would lead to a groundswell of support for a radical redistribution of these civil rights, eventually bringing both communities into direct confrontation with one another.

The NICRA marches sparked off counter-demonstrations led by fundamentalist Protestant preacher the Revd Ian Paisley, whose oratory sent crowds into frenzied hysteria when civil rights marches passed through predominantly Unionist areas. Heavy-handed responses by militant Loyalists and elements of the local Royal Ulster Constabulary (RUC) and the auxiliary Ulster Special Constabulary (USC, or 'B' Specials) provoked further unrest and violence. The reformist impulse behind the initial civil rights marches soon gave way to a mushrooming of militancy. Protestants were jettisoned from NICRA's ranks, and as the province spiralled further into sectarian clashes and civil disorder the Irish Republican Army (IRA) emerged as the cutting edge of Catholic defenderism.

In the heightened atmosphere of the Orange Order's annual marching season during the summer of 1969, nationalist protestors soon found themselves in open conflict with their Protestant neighbours and the police. Widespread sectarian rioting led to the formation of vigilante groups as respective communities clashed on the streets of Northern Ireland. The Troubles, which had lain subdued since the 1920s – with only the occasional glimmer of violence – had been reignited.

Few actions in the Troubles were as momentous as the intervention of British troops. Ordered into the province on 14 August 1969 by Home Secretary James

Cities, towns and villages in Northern Ireland

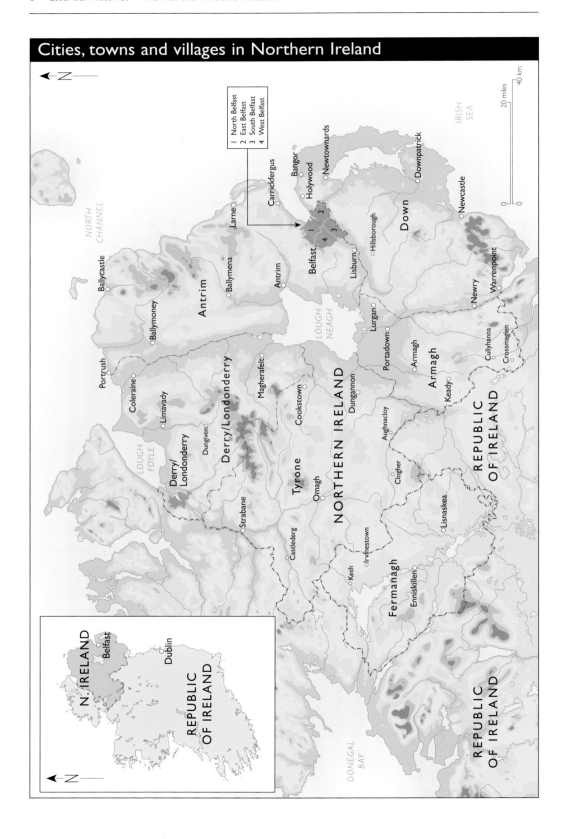

British troops stand guard in Belfast in August 1969.
(© Hulton-Deutsch Collection/Corbis)

Callaghan, following a request by his counterpart in the Northern Ireland government, the troops' task was to 'provide military assistance to the civil power'. Despite its initial peacekeeping posture the British Army was very quickly thrust into the midst of a vicious cycle gripping Northern Ireland's streets. Between 1971 and 1997 Britain saw 770 of its armed forces personnel killed and countless wounded. Approximately 250,000 soldiers qualified for the Northern Ireland clasp of the Army's General Service Medal, and Operation *Banner* became the longest campaign in British military history.

In both political and military terms Operation *Banner* was one of the most significant interventions in modern times. It lasted longer than the Palestine deployment under the British Mandate (1920s to the 1940s) and was infinitely more complex and controversial than the Aden campaign of the 1960s. Politically, many high-profile atrocities – such as the indiscriminate bombing of civilian targets by the various terrorist groups – provoked universal outrage. The knee-jerk reactions of the Security Forces

– made up of the RUC, the locally recruited Ulster Defence Regiment (UDR, later the Royal Irish Regiment Home Service Force), and the British Army – from time to time also served to generate international furore and led to high-profile inquiries. The Parker and Compton Inquiries investigated allegations of the ill-treatment of terrorist suspects, while the Saville Inquiry was appointed to determine responsibility for the events of 'Bloody Sunday', when soldiers shot dead 14 people. These investigations portrayed Britain and her Security Forces in a poor light and, arguably, handed propaganda victories to militant Republicanism.

Many Catholic nationalists joined the IRA, a clandestine organization with a long lineage stretching back to the separatist Fenian Movement and the Irish Republican Brotherhood. In 25 years of violence, Republican paramilitaries (mainly the IRA) were responsible for the murders of over 2,000 people – mostly Protestants. Loyalist paramilitary groups – founded primarily in response to the escalation of Republican violence – killed over 1,018 people, mostly Catholics. The Security Forces were responsible for approximately 363 deaths. Despite the highly sophisticated propaganda campaigns undertaken by terrorists, the sad truth was that most victims of the Troubles were ordinary Protestants and Catholics. Even with the running-down of their respective military campaigns and the onset of the 'peace process' in the 1990s, paramilitaries continued to harass their respective communities with intimidation, threats, violence and murder.

While the 1998 Belfast (or 'Good Friday') Agreement saw the main Unionist and nationalist traditions reach a political accommodation, violence continued on the streets until the decommissioning of IRA weapons in 2005. Power-sharing institutions were finally devolved by the British government to the local Stormont Assembly in a deal between Ian Paisley's Democratic Unionist Party and Gerry Adams' Sinn Féin in May 2007. Meanwhile, it had been announced in July 2006 that due to the winding up of the IRA's campaign the year before – and in the spirit of 'normalization' – the British Army would be terminating Operation *Banner* in July 2007. The statements that Loyalist paramilitaries were ending their terror campaigns served further to bolster the fledgling power-sharing executive at Stormont. All of these developments acted as the adhesive binding together the peace and political processes in the decade after the signing of the Belfast Agreement.

Chronology

1920 Government of Ireland Act passed, partitioning Ireland into North and South

1922 Formation of the RUC

1939–1940 IRA bombing campaign in England

1941 **April–May** Belfast 'Blitz' by the German Luftwaffe

1956 **December** IRA launches its border campaign, Operation *Harvest*

1957 Internment temporarily introduced on both sides of the border

1962 **February** IRA calls a halt to Operation *Harvest* and dumps arms

1964 The Revd Ian Paisley leads protest march into Divis Street in the Falls Road area, sparking off three nights of intense rioting

1965 Ulster Volunteer Force (UVF) formed; former soldier 'Gusty' Spence appointed as its first commander

1966 50th anniversary of the Easter Rising heightens tensions; UVF murders several people across Belfast

1967 Northern Ireland Civil Rights Association (NICRA) formed

1968 **5 October** NICRA march turns violent in Duke Street, Derry/Londonderry

1969 **4 January** People's Democracy march from Belfast to Derry/Londonderry attacked by Loyalists and Ulster Special Constabulary members ('B' Specials) at Burntollet
28 April Northern Ireland's Prime Minister, Terence O'Neill, resigns from office
10 August Rioting in Belfast and Derry/Londonderry
14 August British troops deploy onto Northern Ireland's streets
December IRA splits into Official and Provisional wings

1970 **April** 'B' Specials disbanded; Ulster Defence Regiment formed
3–5 July Falls Road Curfew

1971 **6 February** First British Army soldier, Gunner Robert Curtis, killed by the IRA
9 August Internment reintroduced

1972 **30 January** Soldiers from 1st Battalion, The Parachute Regiment, open fire on civil rights marchers; 27 people are wounded, 14 fatally. It later becomes known as 'Bloody Sunday'
July The IRA detonates 22 bombs across Belfast, killing nine people and injuring hundreds on 'Bloody Friday'; Operation *Motorman* is launched to retake 'no-go' areas

1974 **4 February** The IRA kills 11 (including two young children) when it blows up a coach carrying off-duty soldiers and their families
May Loyalist strike brings down power-sharing experiment
5 October The IRA carries out the bombings of two Guildford pubs, killing four people
21 November The IRA bombs two Birmingham pubs, killing 19

Sinn Féin President Gerry Adams gives a speech in August 2007 commemorating the actions of Republicans in August 1969. He is addressing followers in Bombay Street, the scene of house burnings and violence in the early days of the Troubles. (Aaron Edwards)

1976   **5 January** IRA gunmen execute ten Protestant civilians in Kingsmill, South Armagh; another is wounded
November The IRA reorganizes along cellular lines

1977   Overt military lead in security policy is scaled back in favour of 'police primacy'

1979   **30 March** Airey Neave MP, former Colditz prison escapee and close confidant of Margaret Thatcher, is assassinated by the Irish National Liberation Army (INLA) when a bomb explodes under his car at the House of Commons
27 August Lord Mountbatten, the Queen's cousin and former Chief of the Defence Staff, is blown up by the IRA; 18 British Army soldiers are killed by the IRA in a bomb attack near Warrenpoint

1981   **5 May** Bobby Sands becomes the first IRA hunger striker to die, after

66 days' fasting. Nine other IRA and INLA prisoners follow suit

1982   **6 December** INLA bombs the Droppin' Well pub in Ballykelly, killing 17 people, including 11 off-duty soldiers based in the town

1983   'Supergrass' trials publicly identify leading terrorists

1984   Gerry Adams begins secret dialogue with the British government

1985   **15 November** The Anglo-Irish Agreement is signed between the British and Irish governments; start of 'Ulster Says No' campaign

1987   **8 May** Elite SAS soldiers kill eight IRA terrorists in Loughgall
8 November The IRA detonates a no-warning bomb next to the war memorial in Enniskillen, killing 11 people and injuring 63

1988   **6 March** SAS team kills three IRA terrorists in Gibraltar
16 March Michael Stone, of the Ulster Freedom Fighters (UFF), attacks the funerals of the 'Gibralter Three'
19 March Two off-duty soldiers are abducted and shot dead by the IRA after mistakenly driving into a Republican funeral cortège

1990   **24 October** The IRA uses human bomb tactic, killing several soldiers

1991   **7 February** The IRA mortars 10 Downing Street

1992   **1 July** The Ulster Defence Regiment is amalgamated with The Royal Irish Rangers to form The Royal Irish Regiment
10 August The Ulster Defence Association (UDA), the largest Loyalist paramilitary group, is banned by the British government

This photograph shows the aftermath of the bombing of Omagh in 1998 by the Real IRA, a splinter group. The 500lb no-warning car bomb claimed the lives of 29 people and two unborn children and injured 380. (IWM HU 98383)

1993   **23 October** Shankill Road bombing by the IRA kills nine civilians

1994   **9, 11 & 13 March** The IRA mortars Heathrow Airport
31 August The IRA ends its military hostilities
13 October Loyalist paramilitaries announce a ceasefire

1995   Talks between British and Irish government and paramilitary representatives

1996   **9 February** The IRA detonates a massive bomb in Canary Wharf, London, heralding an end to its ceasefire
30 May Forum Election
15 June The IRA bombs Manchester city centre
July Orange Order parade at Drumcree, County Armagh, leads to widespread civil disturbances in Northern Ireland
7 October The IRA attacks British Army HQ in Lisburn, with two 500lb (227kg) bombs, killing one soldier and injuring 20 other people

1997   **12 February** Lance Bombardier Stephen Restorick is killed by a sniper; he is the last soldier to die in Operation *Banner*
20 July The IRA reinstates its ceasefire

1998   **10 April** The Belfast/Good Friday Agreement is signed
15 August The Real IRA, an ultra-Republican splinter group, explodes a no-warning car bomb in Omagh, County Tyrone, killing 29 people and two unborn children

1999   **29 November** Power-sharing executive appointed
2 December Direct rule ends; power devolved to Stormont

2000   Loyalist feud between the UDA/UFF and the UVF/RHC (Red Hand Commando, a small paramilitary group with close ties to the UVF)

2001   The 'Holy Cross dispute' in Ardoyne, North Belfast, sees British troops once again deployed in a major operation to keep the peace

2002   IRA spy ring uncovered at Stormont, prompting the collapse of the power-sharing executive and suspension of devolution

2005   **28 July** The IRA calls an end to its armed campaign
September Annual Whiterock Orange Order parade in West Belfast ends in the worst rioting in three decades; the IRA decommissions the last of its weapons and explosives

2006   **October** Multi-party talks lead to the St Andrews Agreement

2007   **8 May** Devolution returns to Northern Ireland, as Ian Paisley and Gerry Adams agree to enter a power-sharing executive
31 July Operation *Banner* ends

History, myth and memory in the Troubles

In Ireland, history weighs heavily on the minds of the people. Although admittedly something of a cliché, it is undeniable that there is a tendency for the Irish to remember the far-distant past as strongly as more recent events. And like all monochrome remembrances of the past, there has been a tendency towards the deeply selective. When viewed through the prism of perceived oppression, sacrifice and injustice, these deep-rooted interpretations of the past have led to embittered feelings towards 'the other side'. The myths, memories and symbols of Irish nationalism and Ulster Unionism are self-perpetuating narratives that have served to reinforce the divisions between these two main communities in Northern Ireland. And it is the polarizing effect that this has had that has made the Troubles so enduring.

Conventional wisdom would have us believe that the conflict in Ireland can be distilled into a virulent antagonism between the Irish and the English, but this only masks a deeper-rooted truth that Irish people are – first and foremost – divided among themselves. In the words of Nobel Peace Prize winner and former Social Democratic and Labour Party (SDLP) politician John Hume, '[t]wo major political traditions share the island of Ireland. We are destined by history to live side by side.' The two principal political traditions inhabit 'two lands on one soil', but the longevity of the most recent violent phase of the Northern Ireland conflict indicates how strongly they disagree with one another over the design of the constitutional architecture to be built there.

A towering nationalist figure, however, Hume realized that there was more to it than the crude Republican mantra of 'eight centuries of English subjugation of Ireland'. In the late 1980s and early 1990s Hume embarked on a dialogue to persuade Gerry Adams and other militant Republicans to rethink their dogmatic views on the role of the British government and the position of the Unionist community in Ireland. Ironically, Sinn Féin would eventually overtake Hume's SDLP at the polls in the wake of the signing of the Belfast Agreement in 1998 to become the largest nationalist party in Northern Ireland.

Introducing the gun into Irish politics

Advances in historical scholarship over the years have ensured a more sober analysis of the role of the British government in Ireland, hinting at its steady process of disengagement since before World War I. This has not always been welcome, with Unionists resisting any attempts to force Home Rule upon them, while nationalists have attempted to hasten Britain's total disengagement. In 'Ulster's Solemn League and Covenant' of 1912, 237,368 men and 234,046 women pledged themselves

… in solemn Covenant, throughout this our time of threatened calamity to stand by one another in defending for ourselves and our children our cherished position of equal citizenship in the United Kingdom and in using all means which may be found necessary to defeat the present conspiracy to set up a Home Rule Parliament in Ireland.

The resolve of Unionists to oppose unpopular British policy in Ireland by signing up to a Solemn League and Covenant marked them out as 'Queen's rebels'. Contrary to doctrinaire Republicanism's claim that Unionists are 'misguided Irishmen', they have proved

Table 1. Prime ministers of Northern Ireland, 1921–72

Prime Minister	Entered office	Left office
James Craig	7 June 1921	24 November 1940
John Miller Andrews	27 November 1940	1 May 1943
Basil Brooke	1 May 1943	25 March 1963
Terence O'Neill	25 March 1963	1 May 1969
James Chichester-Clark	1 May 1969	23 March 1971
Brian Faulkner	23 March 1971	30 March 1972

resilient in maintaining the link with Great Britain for a myriad of political, social and economic reasons.

Nevertheless, four years into the Third Home Rule Crisis (1910–14), Unionists were on the back foot. Home Rule looked inevitable. Unionists responded by drilling, first with dummy rifles, and then with thousands of Mannlicher M1904 and Mauser Gew 88 rifles from Germany, and an assortment of handguns landed illegally at the ports of Larne and Donaghadee. They established a paramilitary Ulster Volunteer Force (UVF) commanded by seasoned members of the British officer corps along with a cadre of Army NCOs. An explosive situation built up. Feeling themselves to be under threat too, nationalists formed their own militias, thus preparing the path towards civil war. Unionists accused the British government of betrayal, a mood captured eloquently by Rudyard Kipling in his poem *Ulster 1912*:

> *The blood our fathers spilt,*
> *Our love, our toils, our pains*
> *Are counted us for guilt*
> *And only bind our chains –*
> *Before an Empire's eyes*
> *The traitor claims his price.*
> *What need of further lies?*
> *We are the sacrifice.*

Meanwhile, events beyond Ireland's shores intervened. The assassination of the Archduke Franz Ferdinand by Young Bosnia member Gavrilo Princip in Sarajevo triggered a series of events that would draw Britain into World War I. Irishmen promptly answered the call, serving in their hundreds of thousands, mainly along the Western Front. Local disputes were suspended in favour of what nationalist leader John Redmond called the 'two-fold duty' of all Irishmen – to soldier 'wherever the firing line extends in defence of the right of freedom and religion in this war'.

With the onset of the Anglo-Irish War of Independence of 1919–21, London acted as a constitutional midwife, helping to deliver self-government for North and South by passing the Government of Ireland Act in 1920. It was this legislation that formally partitioned the six north-eastern counties of the ancient nine-county province of Ulster from the 26 south-western counties of Ireland's other three provinces of Leinster, Munster and Connaught. Although Ireland had fallen under English influence from the 12th century onwards, it had only officially been part of the United Kingdom since the Act of Union came into effect in 1801. The Government of Ireland Act established two separate parliaments in Belfast and Dublin, but London held a firm grip on reserved matters like foreign policy, currency, taxation and access to ports in both jurisdictions. It was envisaged that Ireland would eventually be reunited within the framework of the United Kingdom.

The reunification of Ireland proved impossible for a variety of reasons, not least because of the entrenched position adopted by Ulster Unionists, who were reluctant to countenance any further secession from the UK. Instead, following the ceasefire between the British Army and the IRA in 1921, the signing of the Anglo-Irish Treaty established the southern 26 counties as the Irish Free State (Eire), with Dominion status. Northern Ireland rejected rule from Dublin. The Ulster Unionists were also worried about the incursion of IRA 'flying columns' north of the border; the threat of a hostile neighbouring state sponsoring guerrilla forces loomed large in Unionist minds. This existential fear led to the establishment of an internal security apparatus, incorporating the Ulster Special Constabulary in 1920 and the Royal Ulster Constabulary in 1922. The process of state formation, however, was an uphill struggle that took place against the backdrop of violence on the streets. Between 1920 and 1922 approximately 462 people lost their lives; a similar number would die 50 years later in 1972, the single worst year of the more recent Troubles.

The birth of Northern Ireland

The new political entity of Northern Ireland was born out of conflict, as the project of Home Rule for Ireland floundered amid the staunch opposition of Ulster Unionists. Matters were not helped much by the southern state, which under President Eamon de Valera's watchful eye sought to integrate Church and State more closely together into a single nationalist regime in Dublin. De Valera's own staunch Roman Catholic faith left him determined to govern according to exclusively Gaelic traditions. These were absolutely alien to Protestant Unionists, who looked towards the more secular and progressive basis of their union with Great Britain.

Such was the determination to resist incorporation into the southern state that the Unionist administration began to equate its own dominance over local politics, society and culture with the survival of Northern Ireland itself. Orangeism was employed as the adhesive to bind together an uneasy class alliance, and it became the cushion upon which Unionist control and authority rested. When de Valera declared Eire to be 'a Catholic state for Catholic people', Sir James

A mural depicting a charge by members of 36th (Ulster) Division on 1 July 1916. Many of those who answered the call for King and Country had previously been members of the UVF, a paramilitary organization formed in 1912 to oppose Home Rule for Ireland. (Aaron Edwards)

Craig (later Lord Craigavon), Northern Ireland's first prime minister, responded with the (often misquoted) adage about Northern Ireland having 'a Protestant people and a Protestant parliament'. An air of suspicion descended over both parts of the island, marginalizing any popular desire in both jurisdictions for reunification.

In 1948 Irish Taoiseach John A. Costello declared his intent to lead the Free State out of the Commonwealth and towards becoming an independent republic. This in turn provoked extensive lobbying by Northern Ireland Prime Minister Sir Basil Brooke, later Viscount Brookeborough, on behalf of his government. Brooke was the nephew of Viscount Alanbrooke, the former Chief of the Imperial General Staff, and had served in several posts under both Craig and Craig's successor as prime minister of Northern Ireland, John Miller Andrews. Brooke's unflinching commitment to the Union, not to mention his obvious diplomatic skills and charm, ensured that he won the support of British Prime Minister Clement Attlee. Britain's Labour government passed the Ireland Act in 1949, which saw Northern Ireland remain an integral component of the UK.

The border campaign: Operation *Harvest*

However, challenges still remained. The IRA had been a constant threat to the Unionist regime throughout its 50 years of existence. Between 1956 and 1962 it prosecuted a violent campaign – Operation *Harvest* – against the Northern Ireland state, attacking infrastructure targets, such as bridges and the sole BBC transmitter in the province, in a half-hearted bid to end partition. Yet it failed for a number of reasons, not least in that it generated minimal support from the Catholic minority, invited repressive cross-border measures such as internment, and was countered by the political will of the Brookeborough administration.

Speaking in the Stormont Parliament on 18 December 1956, a week after the IRA declared 'our people in the Six Counties have taken the fight to the enemy', the Minister for Home Affairs W. B. Topping said:

Every bullet fired, every bomb thrown, every act of violence which takes place only hammers another nail in the coffin of Republican hopes. It is astonishing that those who are responsible for these acts of violence have not yet learned that bullets cannot shoot beliefs. We believe in Britain and in the British way of life. We are British and British we will remain. (Hon. Members: Hear, hear.)

Security assessments made available to the Stormont government at the time spoke in terms of the calmness displayed by both communities and sharply contrasted this round of violence with that experienced in the 1920s. Within a year the RUC was reporting how 'the life of the community remains largely unaffected'. Several top-level police reports commended Brookeborough

Table 2. Presidents and Taoisigh of the Republic of Ireland

President of the Executive	Entered office	Left office
William T. Cosgrave	6 December 1922	9 March 1932
Eamon de Valera	9 March 1932	29 December 1937

Taoiseach	Entered office	Left office
Eamon de Valera	29 December 1937	18 February 1948
John A. Costello	18 February 1948	13 June 1951
Eamon de Valera	13 June 1951	2 June 1954
John A. Costello	2 June 1954	20 March 1957
Eamon de Valera	20 March 1957	23 June 1959
Sean Lemass	23 June 1959	10 November 1966
Jack Lynch	10 November 1966	14 March 1973
Liam Cosgrove	14 March 1973	5 July 1977
Jack Lynch	5 July 1977	11 December 1979
Charles J. Haughey	11 December 1979	30 June 1981
Garret Fitzgerald	30 June 1981	9 March 1982
Charles J. Haughey	9 March 1982	14 December 1982
Garret Fitzgerald	14 December 1982	10 March 1987
Charles J. Haughey	10 March 1987	11 February 1992
Albert Reynolds	11 February 1992	15 December 1994
John Bruton	15 December 1994	26 June 1997
Bertie Ahern	26 June 1997	6 May 2008
Brian Cowen	7 May 2008	9 March 2011
Enda Kenny	9 March 2011	Incumbent

Fundamentalist Protestant preacher the Revd Ian Paisley led the counter-demonstrations that opposed NICRA marches. Militant Loyalists later blamed Paisley's speeches for propelling them into paramilitarism. (IWM HU 42548)

and his colleagues for consistently urging restraint among their supporters.

In any case the IRA's objectives were unrealistic given the detachment of many nationalists from the political process. Following the resounding failure of the Anti-Partition League earlier in the decade to achieve the abolition of the border in a peaceful manner, constitutional nationalism was quickly supplanted by a more militant Republicanism. An IRA statement released after the first wave of attacks stated:

Out of this national liberation struggle a new Ireland will emerge, upright and free. In that new Ireland we shall build a country fit for all our people to live in. That then is our aim: an independent, united, democratic Irish Republic. For this we shall fight until the invader is driven from our soil and victory is ours.

By launching pre-planned attacks on military and infrastructure targets dotted along the border of Northern Ireland from the 'safe haven' of the Irish Republic, the IRA sought to end partition by physical force. Most commentators writing about this period in Northern Ireland's history tend to dismiss the IRA's border campaign as insignificant, mainly because of the small number of fatalities involved. In total 18 people lost their lives, including 11 IRA men (five were killed in hostilities), and six policemen. Scores were wounded. In light of what was to emerge by the end of the 1960s this is certainly a superficially attractive observation. However, it somewhat misses the point that the Unionist Government was under immense pressure from its grassroots to act against the terrorists.

In a speech at Stormont on 4 July 1957, the same day that an RUC constable was murdered and his colleague seriously injured in an IRA ambush, Unionist MP for Antrim Nat Minford led calls for tougher security measures:

The laws that have been in operation in Cyprus should be enforced here. A man who carries a gun or in any way assists another to carry a gun is not out for the good of the public, and the only punishment should be death.[1]

Although the use of the death penalty was not seriously entertained, the Unionist authorities did turn to tougher measures, under the provisions of the Special Powers Act of 1922. Internment was introduced for the first time in Northern Ireland. The coercive nature of the Unionist response was dictated primarily by the need to prevent anger among grassroots Unionists from boiling over into reprisals. Not for the first time would the Unionist government act to counter angst and threats of vigilantism from among its supporters. The Brookeborough administration's actions were soon complemented by de Valera, whose administration interned IRA suspects south of the border in a bid to offset pressure from London. Within a year 500 suspects had been interned on both sides of the border. Over the next few years the IRA's campaign fizzled out and the organization dumped arms in February 1962.

Loyalist violence: preventive or pre-emptive strikes?

Violence once again returned to Northern Ireland's streets in 1964. This time it was caused by the presence of an Irish tricolour in the window of a shop being used as a headquarters for Westminster election candidate, Republican Liam McMillen. The Revd Ian Paisley, a fundamentalist Presbyterian preacher, led a mob into Divis Street, West Belfast, to remove the flag.

The statue of Sir Winston Churchill peers down imposingly as former Prime Minister Harold Wilson strolls out of the House of Commons with his successor at 10 Downing Street, Conservative leader Edward Heath, on 2 July 1970. Following immediately behind Wilson is James Callaghan, who served as Home Secretary in the late 1960s when the Troubles exploded onto Northern Ireland's streets, and would succeed Wilson as prime minister in the mid-1970s. The Labour Party was given regular updates about the political, socio-economic, and security situation in the province throughout the post-war period, despite claims by Wilson and others that they 'knew nothing about Northern Ireland' before the outbreak of violence. (© Bettmann/Corbis)

Three nights of serious rioting gripped Belfast and the RUC deployed water cannon to quell the disturbances. Scores of Catholic youths later arrested remarked in court that they would not have taken to the streets had it not been for Paisley's intervention.

Anticipating an upsurge in IRA activity, some Unionists resurrected the UVF in 1965 as a means of marshalling vigilante spirit among sections of the Protestant working class. The UVF was a tiny but deadly organization, born out of political intrigue and incubated in the shadows of a Unionist establishment worried about the liberal-leaning policies of Terence O'Neill,

---

1   A major counter-insurgency campaign was fought by Britain's Security Forces in Cyprus between 1955 and 1959. The Greek terrorist group EOKA, led by the ex-Greek army Colonel George Grivas, embarked on a campaign of subversion known as *enosis*, which aimed to reunite the island by force of arms.

Northern Ireland's modernizing fourth prime minister. O'Neill had promised to 'transform the face of Ulster' but he fatally misunderstood the dynamics of sectarianism. Clandestine bomb attacks carried out by the UVF, and subsequently blamed on the IRA, were used as an instrument to force O'Neill's hand towards more coercive anti-IRA measures. Such scare tactics left O'Neill jaded. Worse was to come, however, when the UVF murdered several people across Belfast; this inevitably stoked fear and alienation among the Catholic community.

The UVF recruited across working-class Protestant areas. In an interview conducted by the author with one of its founding members, who later became its second-in-command, he recalled how:

In the mid-1960s you had the perception that there could be an IRA insurrection and that perception was being fostered by senior Unionist politicians – and people like me 'bit'. With the benefit of hindsight now I wouldn't have.

The UVF was symptomatic of a strain of vigilantism that ran through certain sections of the Protestant community. It forced O'Neill from office in 1969.

British ambivalence, Irish malevolence

Harold Wilson's Labour government (1964–70) frequently claimed that they knew very little about Northern Ireland prior to the explosion of violence in August 1969, although for most of the post-war period the British Labour Party had been kept regularly informed of the situation by their smaller sister party, the Northern Ireland Labour Party. In his book *A House Divided*, James Callaghan recalled how when he took over as British Home Secretary in 1967 his despatch box

… contained books and papers on the future of the prison service, the fire service, problems on race relations, a number of questions about the police, children in care and their future, and the reform of the House of Lords – but not a word about Northern Ireland.

The British government's ignorance of the Troubles brewing on the streets of Belfast and Derry/Londonderry was matched only by its ambivalence towards the difficulties facing the Stormont government. Unionists understood only too well the precarious foundations upon which their power rested and they were keen to avoid making concessions. Meanwhile, the Irish government became concerned for the minority community and sought ways to intervene actively on their behalf. Intervention ranged from accommodating northern 'refugees' in camps south of the border, to high-level diplomatic pressure, and the clandestine training and arming of individuals who later went on to form the nucleus of the IRA, carrying out attacks on civilian and military targets.

Brits, Provos and Loyalists

The Security Forces

As the sovereign state responsible for security in Northern Ireland, Britain has always sought to portray its role in the conflict as benign, even going to the extent of declaring itself a 'third party' or 'umpire'. Despite protestations to the contrary, however, Republicans and nationalists regard Britain as one of the principal parties to the conflict. Far from being a 'neutral arbiter' it was motivated mainly by constitutional interests and by the overwhelming desire to insulate itself from what became, in leading strategic theorist M. L. R. Smith's words, 'the most destabilizing issue in British politics for a generation'. Keeping the Irish conflict 'at arm's length' had been the British government's most consistent policy since the formation of Northern Ireland.

It was unsurprising, then, that the prospect of intervening in the province caused considerable consternation within government circles. The Home Secretary, James Callaghan, hoped that the Unionist administration would not need to invoke the 'military aid to the civil power' provision, but was perceptive enough to commission the Ministry of Defence (MoD) to draw up contingency plans for deploying British troops over the Christmas leave period in 1968–69.

2nd Lieutenant David Brough of 1st Battalion, The Parachute Regiment, on patrol in Cupar Street, Belfast, in August 1969, armed with the standard self-loading rifle, or SLR. The British Army's arrival on the streets of Northern Ireland brought with it Saracen armoured personnel carriers, which were to become a familiar sight. (IWM TR 32986)

HRH Prince Andrew, Honorary Colonel of the UDR/Royal Irish Regiment, presents new colours to 3rd Battalion, The Royal Irish Regiment, on 17 June 2000. (IWM HU 98341)

British troops had been deployed on Irish soil before, of course, finally departing the south in the aftermath of the Anglo-Irish War of 1919–21. They had been headquartered in the Curragh near Dublin; after the partitioning of Ireland in 1920 the Army kept a peacetime garrison of several thousand troops in Northern Ireland. That figure swelled from 4,000 to 6,000 upon the outbreak of serious intercommunal violence in mid-August 1969; numbers rose again to 11,243 within a year. Based in Lisburn, Headquarters Northern Ireland (HQNI) became the operational hub for all military operations in the province. In August 1969, 39 (Infantry) Brigade was established, responsible for Belfast and the eastern part of the province; 8 (Infantry) Brigade took over operational responsibility for the north and west of the province in January 1970, and 3 (Infantry) Brigade oversaw operations in Northern Ireland's southern region.

Northern Ireland presented a wholly novel challenge for British troops. Reflecting on his time as Commanding Officer of 3rd Battalion, The Parachute Regiment

(3 Para), in South Armagh during the 1970s, Peter Morton observed how 'soldiering in Northern Ireland is certainly not about aggression, nor fatalism, and indeed many would argue that it is not really soldiering at all'. The British Army tended to rely on tried-and-tested methods of dealing with civil unrest and violence. The troops who were initially deployed to Derry/Londonderry and Belfast advanced to trouble spots in box formation, a type of colonial policing technique that afforded troops the opportunity to outmanoeuvre rioters and stop violence before it had a chance to escalate.

The Army arrived on the streets, therefore, with limited knowledge of the Troubles facing them, and they depended disproportionately on the experience of members of both the RUC and (from 1970) the new, locally recruited part-time Ulster Defence Regiment (UDR), who were more familiar with the nuances underpinning the conflict. As one former Royal Engineers soldier remarked, 'They were there all the time. It was their home. We were just visitors.' The RUC had 3,000 officers in 1969 and could call on a further 1,500 members of the Ulster Special Constabulary (USC), known as the 'B' Specials, in dire situations. Although they were routinely armed, there were few violent incidents. However, as their reaction to the trouble in Divis Street in 1964 had demonstrated, they had little public-order training. In the case of the USC there was a general lack of discipline, particularly among the reservist 'C' Specials. Following the 1969 Hunt Report's recommendations, the USC was abolished and replaced by the UDR.

The Provisional IRA

Despite the military failure of its border campaign, the IRA extended its insurgency to the realm of political subversion and agitation as a means of preparing the ground for future action against the north. Many of those who later joined the IRA after street disturbances would contend that they were propelled into paramilitary ranks because of the context of the time, which made 'ordinary people' do 'extraordinary things'. In an interview with the author, one former IRA member said he joined its ranks when state opposition to civil rights marches cut off the means of peacefully registering protest. 'We tried the force of argument; it didn't work so … it had to be the argument of force.' This was a view shared by a growing number of men and women who recognized that in order to bring about 'a fairer society', things had to be 'deconstructed'. For the former IRA member, 'the only vehicle that could possibly bring that about was the IRA'.

The IRA was reborn out of the ashes of Bombay Street, a small, close-knit Catholic community in the shadow of the Clonard Monastery in West Belfast, which was razed to the ground during severe rioting in August 1969. While before there had been a handful of IRA members across Belfast, what structure there was had little command-and-control capability, and weapons were practically non-existent. By the end of the year the IRA had split into two organizations and had mushroomed in size to almost 1,000 members. Following a meeting of the ruling IRA Army Council, dissidents in favour of a more proactive defence of beleaguered Catholic communities made their position known through the media. At a Sinn Féin/IRA *Ard Feis* (main meeting) in January 1970 the Republican movement formally split. Those who remained behind became known as the Officials and those dissidents who left became known as the Provisionals.

In walking away from existing IRA structures, the Provisionals faced the momentous task of building up a new underground organization. According to evidence he gave at the Saville Inquiry into Bloody Sunday, Martin McGuinness estimated that the Provisional IRA in the city of Derry/Londonderry was a small unit, with only 40–50 active members in 1970–71. In an interview with the author, a former leading member of the organization's Belfast Brigade, Tommy Gorman, recalled that

The IRA drew on history to justify its resort to 'armed struggle'. This memorial in Derry/Londonderry City Cemetery commemorates the 1981 hunger strikers. (Aaron Edwards)

although the Provisionals attracted new recruits, for every 300 members in a company, only about five were active:

It was in a pretty bad state. I think in Divis Street that night [1969] there were a couple of short arms and a sub-machine gun. But … at that time it was moribund. And it was in the influx of new recruits and all these older people who had been retired and had gone out back to their farms or something and had suddenly reappeared again and gave us some sort of structure. And it was based on the British Army [structure]. You had companies, battalions and brigades. And companies were based on geographical areas so security was pretty lax. And with the influx of so many new volunteers anybody can sneak in with the rush.

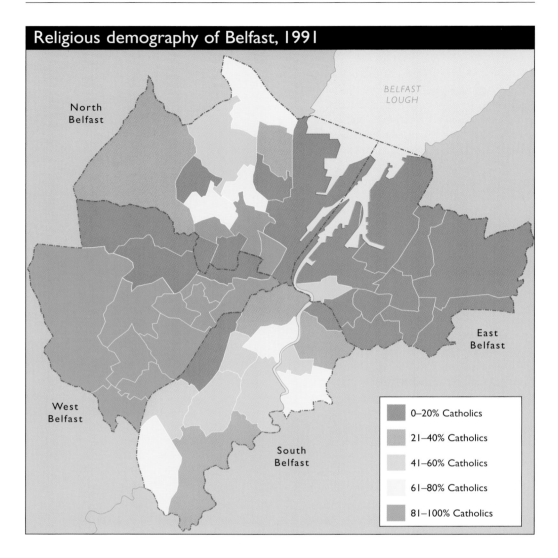

Religious demography of Belfast, 1991

BELFAST LOUGH

North Belfast

East Belfast

West Belfast

South Belfast

■	0–20% Catholics
■	21–40% Catholics
■	41–60% Catholics
□	61–80% Catholics
■	81–100% Catholics

Networks of police, Army and security services informers – or 'touts' as they became known in local parlance – soon penetrated the IRA from top to bottom. This became one of the main reasons why the British state was later able to inflict a strategic defeat on the organization.

IRA members came from a variety of backgrounds, though most of the raw recruits, like Gorman, came from working-class areas. Few, if any, had prior military training and the majority joined the IRA following a brush with street violence in their local neighbourhoods. Several were also hardened criminals, who found themselves caught up in Republican militancy because of their expertise in procuring funds through illicit means. As J. Bowyer Bell observed in his seminal study on the IRA, *The Secret Army*, '[f]ew Irish rebels are as skilled as the professional soldier – although the protraction of the struggle has meant a rise in standards, standards constantly eroded by losses, lack of training, the needs of the moment, and the failure of corporate memory'. Nonetheless, the IRA was accomplished at portraying its membership as being 'principled soldiers of Ireland'. In its internal Code of Conduct, known to rank-and-file members as the *Green Book*, it

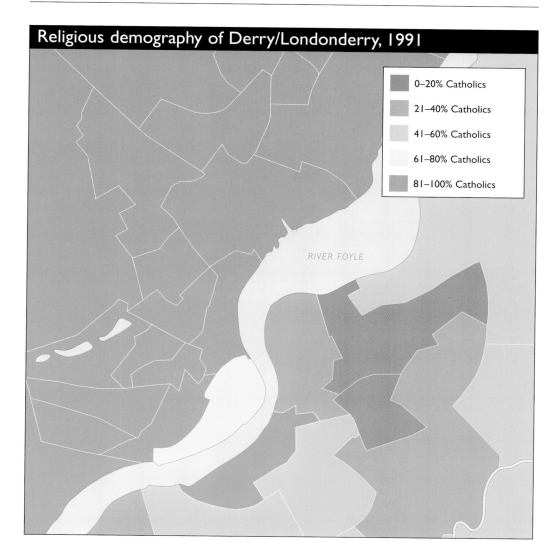

Religious demography of Derry/Londonderry, 1991

0–20% Catholics
21–40% Catholics
41–60% Catholics
61–80% Catholics
81–100% Catholics

RIVER FOYLE

warned that '[a]ny Volunteer who brings the Army into disrepute by his/her behaviour may be guilty of a breach of his/her duties and responsibilities as a Volunteer in *Óglaigh na hÉireann* and may be dismissed'.

In terms of weapons and explosives the IRA began as a poorly equipped and ill-disciplined organization. A Provisional IRA member interviewed by the Saville Inquiry recalled how

... [t]he weaponry was very ancient to say the least. The Creggan and Bogside units would each have had something like a Thompson [submachine gun], an M1 Carbine, a couple

of .303s. There may have been a couple of revolvers as well.

Despite these drawbacks, the IRA would soon emerge as one of the world's most sophisticated guerrilla movements. Remarkably, this transformation would take place within a matter of months.

Loyalist paramilitaries

Loyalist paramilitarism was a small-scale affair at the outset of the Troubles. It coalesced mainly around the secretive UVF,

The Ulster Volunteer Force emerged in 1965 to counter the perceived threat posed by the IRA. It murdered almost 500 people during the Troubles. (Fred Hoare)

re-established in November 1965. By 1971, Loyalist paramilitary ranks had ballooned with the formation of the Ulster Defence Association (UDA). The UDA was a huge, unwieldy organization, boasting over 40,000 members by the mid-1970s. Some of its more militant members established an armed wing, the Ulster Freedom Fighters, which killed approximately 259 people between 1971 and 2002. Unionist politicians were worried at the prospect of vigilantism; others, like Stormont Minister for Home Affairs Bill Craig, sought to harness paramilitary muscle for their own political purposes. Protestant militancy soon emerged as a formidable force in Northern Ireland politics.

The UVF portrayed itself as a 'counter-terrorist outfit' during the Troubles. Indeed many of its key members had previous military experience in the British armed forces, with its first commander Augustus 'Gusty' Spence having served in anti-EOKA operations in Cyprus in the late 1950s. One former member had even served in the ranks of the Special Air Service, fighting communist terrorists in Malaya. In the early

1970s several UVF members also belonged to the Territorial Army. It was not long before the UVF began to organize itself along British Army lines. As one former leader revealed in an interview with the author:

The UVF was formed on a British brigade structure of three battalions, Belfast, Mid Ulster and East Antrim. The idea for the East Antrim Battalion [was that] people believed that it wasn't about the interfaces, it was about the constitution, the future of Northern Ireland, so the UVF was not formed to deal with interfaces, it was formed because they believed there was a sell out, there was a rebellion which had to be stopped. Whether you were from the Shankill or East Antrim you had the one enemy – the IRA. Indeed the nationalist community [more broadly were considered the enemy], as most UVF volunteers didn't distinguish between the IRA and those they fought for.

The UVF was a ruthless terrorist organization, responsible for approximately 458 deaths between 1966 and 2002: 84 per cent of its victims were civilians, 10 per cent were other Loyalists, 5 per cent were Republicans and 1 per cent were Security Forces personnel. The Loyalists were to prove as ruthless in their violence as their Republican enemies.

Politics in the streets

Formed in 1967, the Northern Ireland Civil Rights Association (NICRA) sought a redistribution of employment, housing, and voting rights for all. Mostly made up of Catholic nationalists, Republicans, agnostic socialists and liberals, NICRA initially had a handful of Protestants in its ranks; however, following a violent clash between marchers and police in Derry/Londonderry's Duke Street on 5 October 1968 most Protestants left. NICRA, in historian and author Bob Purdie's words, 'underestimated the problems which its slight Republican taint would cause'. Many civil rights marches were already illegal, but the withdrawal of law-abiding Protestant citizens – whose presence gave the movement a degree of political protection – did not deter it from using dangerously confrontational tactics to draw attention to its cause. Nor did it deter its leaders from demanding concessions – such as the abolition of the Special Powers Act and the disbandment of the 'B' Specials – from the Stormont administration.

In the view of Loyalists like Billy Mitchell, interviewed by the author, NICRA was really only seeking 'civil rights for Catholics'. Mitchell, a committed Paisleyite in the 1960s and 1970s, had joined the UVF in 1970, rising through its ranks to become the organization's alleged leader by the middle of the decade. He described how Unionist politicians repeatedly warned Loyalists that an IRA threat existed in

The Northern Ireland Civil Rights Association took to the streets to demand an end to discrimination in jobs, housing and the electoral franchise. (IWM HU 55865)

2nd Lieutenant James Daniell and two riflemen of
1st Battalion, The Royal Green Jackets, enjoy cups of tea
and biscuits prepared by a local resident in Cupar Street
in the Catholic Falls Road area in December 1969.
Following the outbreak of violence in summer 1969,
British troops were initially welcomed by Catholics as
protectors; however, this 'honeymoon period' lasted only
a matter of months. (IWM TR 32994-1)

the 1960s; Republicans, they were told,
had infiltrated the ranks of the civil rights
movement. Evidence for such claims was
readily available. The IRA's Chief of Staff, Sean
Garland, had been arrested in Dublin in 1966,

along with a document that outlined how
the IRA intended to subvert trades unions
and other bodies established to lobby for
socio-economic reform, and prompt them
to push for a united Ireland. It was just what
Paisley had been warning about. Suddenly the
theoretical threat posed by the IRA became a
real one in the minds of many Unionists.
NICRA became tainted by association.

What made matters worse was that the
tribalism associated with marching was
deeply ingrained in the psyche of both
communities. By insisting on walking
through majority Protestant areas, NICRA

actually fanned the flames of resentment between the two communities. Many Protestants observing the civil rights movement just could not understand why Catholics were seeking a radical redistribution of rights that most working-class people – of whatever creed – did not themselves enjoy. Furthermore, Protestants saw the attacks on the RUC and the 'B' Specials as a direct attack on *their* state.

Violence increased markedly during the hot summer of 1969 as Orange Order marches got under way. Of the nine people who lost their lives in July and August, six were killed by the RUC, one by the 'B' Specials, one by Loyalists and another by Republicans. The atmosphere became electric. The use of machine guns by the RUC – particularly in enclosed urban areas – bordered on recklessness and alarmed many people, including politicians in London. Nine-year-old Patrick Rooney was shot and killed in his bed by a .30-calibre bullet, fired from a Browning M1919A4 machine gun mounted on top of an RUC Shorland armoured car. One eyewitness later interviewed by the author said that the use of such weaponry by the police led many local people to believe that 'an even greater loss of life had been incurred' than was actually the case. Although the death toll was surprisingly low given the sheer intensity of the street violence, perception was everything, and it fed a vicious cycle. Sectarian confrontation fanned the flames of violence as politics once again returned to the streets of Northern Ireland.

The British Army arrives

At approximately 1635 hours on the afternoon of 14 August 1969, a request was made by the RUC's Inspector General for the immediate deployment of troops to support the civil power in Northern Ireland. Home Secretary James Callaghan received the message from Whitehall mid-flight as he made his way back to Wiltshire from a meeting with Prime Minister Harold Wilson.

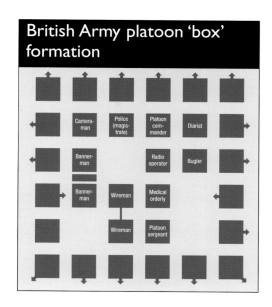

British Army platoon 'box' formation

Radioing back to London, he quickly granted permission for the use of troops.

The first unit deployed to Derry/Londonderry was 1st Battalion, The Prince of Wales's Own Regiment of Yorkshire, with orders to relieve exhausted members of the RUC and 'B' Specials and to keep the peace between two warring communities. A statement issued by the British government at the time read:

The GOC [General Officer Commanding] N. Ireland has been instructed to take all necessary steps, acting impartially between citizen and citizen, to restore law and order. Troops will be withdrawn as soon as this is accomplished. This is a limited operation and during it troops will remain under the direct and exclusive control of the GOC who will continue to be responsible to the UK Government.

That night, no sooner had violence been brought under control in Derry/Londonderry than it flared up in Belfast. On the night of 14/15 August the sound of gunfire and exploding bombs in the province's two main cities could be heard amid an upsurge in intercommunal rioting between Protestants and Catholics. Following a desperate appeal to Callaghan for further troop deployment

The Falls Road, 1970. British troops wear respirators to protect them against the noxious fumes of CS gas. Eyewitnesses said that thick clouds of smoke could be seen billowing over the areas worst hit by intercommunal violence. (IWM HU 55875)

by Gerry Fitt, the Independent Republican Westminster MP for West Belfast, the Home Secretary remarked, 'Gerry, I can get the Army in but it's going to be a devil of a job to get it out.'

As Fitt's appeal demonstrated, Catholics welcomed the soldiers with open arms when they first arrived in August 1969. Within a matter of weeks the GOC Northern Ireland,

Sir Ian Freeland, conceded at a press conference that if a political solution uniting Belfast and London could not be found, then 'the honeymoon period could finish in matter of hours. Our soldiers, in between the rival factions in Belfast, might become the target of both sides.' Freeland's observations proved accurate. The relationship soon soured, first in Derry/Londonderry and then in Belfast, as the Army was accused of standing aside while Loyalist militants ransacked and burned Catholic homes.

Following a meeting between influential members of the Catholic community, which included Fitt and Stormont MP Paddy Devlin,

British troops were deployed to Belfast on 15 August 1969 to keep the peace between Protestants and Catholics. (John White, courtesy of Frankie Quinn)

The Army had deployed to the province with little knowledge of the nature of the conflict between Protestants and Catholics. To address this deficit they applied tried-and-tested techniques from colonial theatres in an attempt to quell the violence. The columns of soldiers marching up Shipquay Street in Derry City in box formation illustrates this well; so too does the apocryphal tale of a banner being unfurled on the streets with instructions in Arabic to 'disperse or we fire' emblazoned on it. Public-order training was an integral component of the Army's Internal Security doctrine at the time.

Two weeks after he authorized the deployment of troops, Callaghan arrived in Belfast for talks with Northern Ireland's prime minister, James Chichester-Clark, on the package of reforms negotiated between the two governments in London and Belfast. Callaghan visited the areas worst hit by rioting, reassuring Catholics on a visit to the Bogside in Derry/Londonderry that he would 'bend all his endeavours' towards ensuring that all citizens of Northern Ireland would enjoy justice and equality and freedom from fear. When he returned again a few weeks later he announced the findings of the Hunt Report, which recommended the disbandment of the 'B' Specials and the disarmament of the RUC. It was too little, too late. Catholics were soon calling for more than reform of the state; many were

Callaghan issued a press release in which he made it clear that 'General Freeland had assured him that by means of the peace line and in other ways the Army would afford all reasonable protection for whatever period it was necessary'. Indeed, the Army attempted to reach an agreement at a local level with both communities about dismantling barricades. Nevertheless, the intensity of the intercommunal violence made establishing a 'peace line' – makeshift barbed-wire fences, later to become permanent walls – the only way to keep both sides apart, especially in Belfast where Protestants and Catholics lived in close proximity.

Police come under sustained attack by rioters in Belfast. A Shorland armoured car has just been petrol-bombed. The Shorland, a Land Rover-based armoured car equipped with a .30-calibre machine-gun turret, was later replaced by the Hotspur. (Fred Hoare)

even beginning to look to the cutting edge of the IRA for a solution to the problem.

The violence escalates

The short-lived Community Relations Commission (CRC) estimated that in 1971 alone 2,069 families moved out of their homes across Belfast because of political violence. The areas worst affected included the predominantly Catholic districts of Ardoyne and Clonard, where 363 families left, and the Grosvenor Road and Roden Street area, where 225 families sought refuge elsewhere. Most families who moved out of these areas were Protestant, while in Ballysillan the overwhelming outflow was made up of Catholic families. The South Belfast area of Suffolk was worst hit: over 88 per cent of those who moved out were Protestant. The CRC report concluded that the biggest population shift in Western Europe since 1945 was caused by an 'overpowering sense of insecurity and fear'.

However, these figures were dwarfed by the population movement in Derry/Londonderry. In 1971 there were 8,459 Protestants living in the west side of the city; by 1981 that figure had dropped to 2,874, and by 1991 it had plummeted again to 1,407. This represented a staggering population decline of 83.4 per cent.

Some Unionists thought that the Stormont government had lost control of the situation and was allowing the province to slip into chaos and anarchy. In a letter to Prime Minister James Chichester-Clark on 27 September 1969 Dr Norman Laird, the Stormont MP for Belfast St Anne's, summed up the feelings of his supporters when he warned:

I am quite satisfied the Cabinet does not know the extent of the very bitter resentment throughout the Country. Loyalists have been extremely patient and tolerant but the limit of toleration is not far off, and if the loyalists really rise up in anger the resulting explosion all over the Country will make what has happened so far look like a child's picnic.

Such apocalyptic language was commonplace among the Unionist grassroots. Something had to be done, and quickly. A new front now opened up as Unionists began to establish vigilante organizations.

From counter-insurgency to internal security

The tempo of armed conflict in Northern Ireland fluctuated according to the bigger political picture. Violence peaked at times of great intercommunal strife and troughed at times when breakthroughs were widely thought to have been made on the constitutional front. Throughout Operation *Banner* the Army was issued with a number of directives from Whitehall, which firmly subordinated military operations to wider policy goals. Moreover, the campaign also ebbed and flowed as the threat from terrorism evolved. In 1969 and 1970 the Army kept a tentative peace, while the decision by the IRA to go on the offensive in 1971 saw British troops respond with a counter-insurgency drive against the insurgents. With the advent of 'police primacy' in 1977, the Army's role would be scaled back over the remaining 30 years of Operation *Banner* to one of providing military support for the RUC in counter-terrorist operations.

Countering insurgency

The violence that gripped Northern Ireland in 1971 posed a number of difficulties for military commanders on the ground. Lieutenant-General Sir Harry Tuzo, General Officer Commanding (GOC) Northern Ireland between 1971 and 1973, was a seasoned soldier more accustomed to operating in colonial theatres like Borneo than the domesticated surroundings of Northern Ireland. In colonial outposts the Army knew who the enemy was, why he was the enemy, and above all how to apply the right amount of military force in order to defeat him. In Belfast and Derry/Londonderry the centre of gravity had shifted and it was proving infinitely

General Sir Harry Tuzo at Sovereign's Parade at the Royal Military Academy Sandhurst in 1973. Tuzo was General Officer Commanding Northern Ireland between 1971 and 1973. Behind him stands the then-Commandant, Major-General Robert Ford. (Courtesy of the Sandhurst Collection)

more difficult to win over the 'hearts and minds' of the local Catholic population, especially when it was so utterly opposed to the Unionist administration. The IRA, backed up by the newly swollen ranks of disaffected nationalist youths, ensured that the military's counter-insurgency tactics soon floundered.

In coming face-to-face with the civil disobedience engulfing the province, Tuzo was determined to tackle the threat head on. He dismissed criticism from Unionists in border areas that troops were not doing enough to protect them or that the Security Forces had all but adopted a defensive posture. 'Anti-guerrilla tactics,' he wrote at the time, 'often appear in this light, especially in a civilised community where the rule of common law still has a part to play'. Tuzo concluded perceptively, '[t]he hard fact is that in guerrilla war the enemy holds the initiative for large parts of the time

This mural on the Falls Road depicts the events of 3–5 July 1970, when the Army imposed a curfew on the area. Many of the tactics used by troops, such as stop-and-search, had been used extensively in colonial policing settings. (Aaron Edwards)

and information is the key to his defeat'. Without the support of key sections of the population the flow of information soon dried up.

In the Bogside, like in so many ghettoized areas across the province, the Catholic population had now turned against Tuzo's soldiers. The 'honeymoon period' enjoyed by the troops following their initial deployment in 1969 ended abruptly and without any real prospect of reconciliation. Instead of being treated to cups of tea and sandwiches by Catholic housewives, British soldiers were now greeted with gunfire, bombs and widespread civil disorder.

Early attempts to quell rioting – or 'aggro' as soldiers called it – were clumsy. Large-scale cordon-and-search operations served only to alienate Catholic working-class opinion. Furthermore, the Army's ability to respond to the embryonic IRA propaganda campaign

was amateurish, and, in the words of one former staff officer, speaking to the author, it 'simply had not been thought through'. In all this General Tuzo was working at a disadvantage. The Stormont and London governments were constantly quarrelling over security matters. The confusing political signals made it much more difficult for the soldiers operating on the ground whose advice Stormont ministers were reluctant to accept. This was to have tragic repercussions in the early 1970s.

In a cordon-and-search operation known popularly ever since as 'the Falls Road curfew', Tuzo's predecessor General Ian Freeland reluctantly ordered soldiers into the Lower Falls in Belfast on 3 July 1970 to search for IRA weapons. In the unfolding drama, rioting broke out, the air became thick with plumes of smoke billowing from burning vehicles and homes, and soldiers fired numerous CS gas canisters to disperse the crowd. The CS gas drifted into residential homes, choking their occupants, many of whom were desperately trying to carve out an ordinary existence for themselves amid the chaos. Matters were made infinitely worse when a curfew was imposed, playing straight into the IRA's hands.

As a result, Tuzo and his deputy, Major-General Robert Ford, soon found themselves confronted with the perennial difficulty of drawing out the insurgents into a clash with the Security Forces, especially since they were now firmly embedded in a community who began to see the IRA as their defenders. However, this was by no means the same story across Northern Ireland. The majority Protestant population wished to maintain the link with Great Britain and they generally supported the Security Forces. Yet for a sizeable minority, concentrated in areas hardened by generations of anti-British sentiment, the fight was less clear cut. The conundrum facing Tuzo and Ford in Northern Ireland was to take over a quarter of a century to solve.

Although the British Army's own reservoir of intellectual thought on counter-insurgency was extensive, it was a direct product of the Army's involvement in military interventions since 1945, in Palestine, Malaya, Kenya, Cyprus and Aden, with varying levels of success and failure. The Army's own guide to best practice for its commanders – what it calls 'doctrine' – characterized insurgents in the following terms:

The insurgent is usually careless of death. He has no mental doubts, is little troubled by humanitarian sentiments, and is not moved by slaughter and mutilation. His upbringing and standard of living make him well fitted to hardship. He requires little sustenance and comfort, and can look after himself. The insurgent has a keen and practised eye for country and has the ability to move across it, at speed, on his feet. He is capable of being trained to use modern and complicated weapons to good effect.

The Army may have been well equipped to fight an arduous guerrilla war in these colonial contexts, but in the heart of British cities such as Belfast and Derry/Londonderry it was a different matter. The Army's carelessness, mixed with the Irish penchant

Major-General (later General Sir) Robert Ford was Commander Land Forces Northern Ireland between 1971 and 1973. He was present on 'Bloody Sunday' and was later vilified by nationalists for his role on the day. (Courtesy of the Sandhurst Collection)

for drawing strength from several hundred years of perceived injustice, contributed to an explosive situation.

Republican operations soon became more aggressive. In contrast to the defensive posture adopted in the summer of 1969, in January 1971 the Provisional IRA Army Council issued the authorization to conduct offensive operations against the Security Forces. The first soldier to lose his life was Gunner Robert Curtis, who was ambushed by an IRA unit commanded by Billy Reid from the New Lodge Road, on 6 February 1971. Gunner Curtis's troop was on public order duty, trying to prevent a mob from attacking people at the New Lodge/Tiger's Bay interface. The crowd broke up to allow an IRA gunman to throw a nail bomb, which was closely followed by a long burst of automatic fire. The crowd then re-formed to prevent soldiers from giving chase. Four of

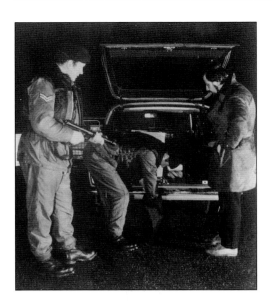

Soldiers from 3rd Battalion, The Ulster Defence Regiment, manning a Vehicle Check Point (VCP) in County Down in January 1972. The UDR was formed in 1970, becoming an integral component of counter-terrorist operations in the province. (IWM MH 30540)

Gunner Curtis's comrades were also injured. Reid was later killed when he attempted to ambush a British Army patrol on 15 May 1971, ironically at the corner of Curtis Street/Academy Street, behind St Anne's Cathedral.

The IRA began to target off-duty soldiers. The brutal murders of three young Scottish soldiers (two of them brothers) aged 17, 18 and 23 on 10 March 1971 at Ligoniel, North Belfast, graphically illustrated the extent to which the IRA was determined to 'blood' its volunteers. Lured to their deaths by two female IRA members after a night out, each of the young men was shot in the back of the head by gunmen as they relieved themselves by the side of a quiet country road. It was not to be the last time that the 'honey-trap' tactic was used by the IRA. On 23 March 1973 female terrorists again lured four off-duty soldiers to a house on the Antrim Road, with the pretext of attending a party. No sooner had the women left the house than IRA gunmen burst in and frogmarched the soldiers to one of the bedrooms, where they were all told to kneel down facing the bed. The gunmen then opened fire with an automatic rifle. Two soldiers were killed instantly and the third died of his wounds a short time later; the fourth soldier miraculously survived. The IRA repeated the 'honey-trap' ploy again in 1981, when one soldier was murdered and another seriously wounded in similar circumstances. Such cold-blooded and premeditated acts had echoes of the ruthlessness that characterized the Jewish insurgency against British forces in Palestine in the 1940s.

By Easter 1971, the Army was dealing with mass rioting, endless blast and nail bombings, the erection of barricades and countless contacts with IRA and Loyalist gunmen on a daily basis. In its first deployment in the Lower Falls area, 3rd Battalion, The Royal Anglian Regiment, experienced a particularly busy tour. Its Tactical Area of Responsibility bordered the Protestant Shankill to the north, the Grosvenor in the south, the Upper Falls/Springfield Road to the west, and Millfield to the east. As a flavour of what units on emergency tour could expect, on 19 April 1971 alone, 177 shots were fired at the battalion; in its four months in-theatre, it suffered four fatalities and 36 wounded.

Countering such violence was largely undertaken on an ad hoc basis dictated by operational circumstances. However, from time to time the Army conducted major operations as directed from London, but with considerable political pressure exerted from Stormont. Perhaps the most counter-productive of these was internment (known by its military codename Operation *Demetrius*), which saw province-wide sweeps to capture senior members of the IRA. In an interview with the author, one former staff officer present at a briefing of 39 (Infantry) Brigade commanders on the morning of 9 August 1971 recalled overhearing one senior officer tell his subordinates in confident mood that 'today is the beginning of the end for the IRA' and that 'without the head, the body will simply thrash around and eventually die'. The same officer talked

Members of 1st Battalion, The Parachute Regiment, in Derry/Londonderry on 'Bloody Sunday'. Within the space of 30 minutes 27 people had been shot by the Paras. Thirteen people died instantly and another two weeks later. The events of that day were a turning point in the Troubles. (Fred Hoare)

Father Edward Daly waves a white flag to clear a route through the streets of Derry/Londonderry on 'Bloody Sunday' as the lifeless body of Jackie Duddy is carried by local people. (Fred Hoare)

to a sergeant from the Parachute Regiment at Palace Barracks shortly after the initial round-ups, who made the telling observation that 'for every one we picked up we have recruited ten for the IRA'.

Initially hostile to internment, the Army nonetheless set about implementing the political will of both the Stormont and London governments in arresting and detaining suspects. However, there were signs that within six months, Headquarters Northern Ireland was warming to the idea of relaxing the security measure in order to curry favour with the Catholic minority, as the following secret letter to No. 10 Downing Street made clear:

The Army recognise that the political initiative which is taken with the object of recapturing the confidence of the Catholic community, while retaining that of the Protestants, will have to include some move on internment if the initiative is to stand any chance of succeeding – and it is of course very much in the Army's interest that it should succeed.

Most evidence suggests that the Army was politically sensitive to the non-military remedies proposed to end the violence;

however, there remains a question mark over the extent to which it could hope to influence government policy. The Army, like other elements of the Security Forces, were the servants of their political masters. In any case, many IRA leaders had slipped the net and internment soon became an unmitigated disaster. Unsurprisingly, perhaps, violence again escalated.

One of the Army's most controversial operations was that undertaken by

Corporal W. C. 'Billy' Hatton, who later won the Queen's Gallantry Medal, detains a rioter on Bloody Sunday. (Fred Hoare)

'Bloody Sunday', The Bogside, 30 January 1972

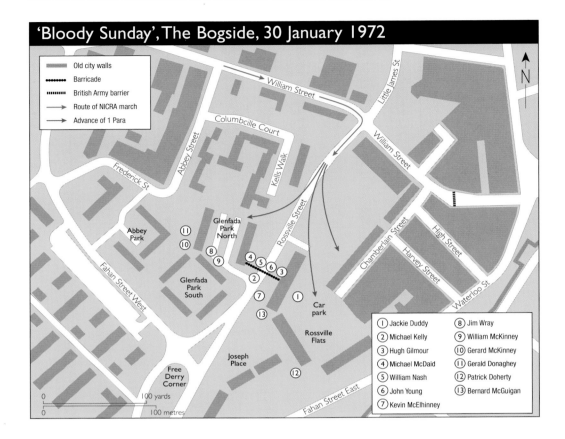

Legend:
- Old city walls
- Barricade
- British Army barrier
- Route of NICRA march
- Advance of 1 Para

Key figures:
1. Jackie Duddy
2. Michael Kelly
3. Hugh Gilmour
4. Michael McDaid
5. William Nash
6. John Young
7. Kevin McElhinney
8. Jim Wray
9. William McKinney
10. Gerard McKinney
11. Gerald Donaghey
12. Patrick Doherty
13. Bernard McGuigan

1st Battalion, The Parachute Regiment, on 30 January 1972. Later known as 'Bloody Sunday', the arrest operation was launched to round up suspected ringleaders of the violence that frequently accompanied illegal civil rights marches. Within 30 minutes of 1 Para entering the largely Catholic Bogside, 27 people had been shot, 14 fatally. The episode quickly soured relations between the Army and the nationalist community, providing a 'recruiting sergeant' for the IRA. The very use of the label 'Bloody Sunday' conjured up parallels with the Black and Tans' shooting of 12 Irish civilians in Croke Park, Dublin, on Sunday 21 November 1920.

Gun and bomb attacks increased in frequency across Northern Ireland after Bloody Sunday. In 1972–73 there were over 15,650 shootings and 2,360 bomb explosions. In 1972 alone 497 people were killed as a result of the Troubles and 4,876 injured. Fourteen per cent

of these deaths were concentrated in North Belfast, with the remainder spread evenly across Belfast, Derry/Londonderry City and South Armagh.

Another dimension to the Troubles brewing in Northern Ireland during the early 1970s was the round of tit-for-tat bombings and shootings between Loyalist and Republican paramilitaries. Attacks on pubs and social clubs became the preferred course of action for all terrorist groups operating in the province. Deep-seated residential segregation made it relatively straightforward for rival groups to attack their perceived enemies without endangering those 'on their side'. Loyalists were cruder in their targeting than Republicans, in large part because, as they argued, the IRA 'did not wear a uniform'. The emergence of the sociopathic 'Shankill Butchers' gang was a direct response to the climate of fear that prompted ordinary individuals to become killers. At a tactical level Loyalist paramilitaries did not possess the same degree of technical sophistication that marked the Provisional IRA out as a deadly terrorist organization. However, this made them no less dangerous.

The Provisional IRA bombing campaign

Bombs were the IRA's main weapon of choice. There were countless incidents throughout the 38 years of Operation *Banner* involving the use of explosives (from fertilizer bombs to Semtex and C4), Improvised Explosive Devices (IEDs), mortars, blast bombs, under-car booby-trap bombs and mines. In the early 1970s the IRA's explosives were typically constructed using over-the-counter ingredients. As one former bomb-maker revealed in an interview with the author:

In the initial parts of the struggle all of our explosives were homemade. We called it co-op mix because you could have got it in the corner shop. There were different mixes. Benzene mixes, diesel mix with fertilizer and stuff like that …

The devastating impact that explosions were to have on individuals was unparalleled; however, the IRA also decided to attack commercial targets, as a means of inflicting severe economic pressure on the British taxpayer.

In response the Army formed 321 Explosive Ordnance Disposal (EOD) Company, mainly from the ranks of the Royal Army Ordnance Corps. Between 1969 and 1992, 321 EOD Company dealt with over 40,000 emergency calls, averaging about 40 per week. In 1991 the organization defused an 8,000lb (3,629kg) proxy bomb, the biggest bomb ever made safe in Northern Ireland, near the Annaghmartin Permanent Vehicle Checkpoint (PVC). The first Army Technical Officer (ATO) to be killed was 29-year-old Captain David Stewartson, who was blown up attempting to defuse a bomb on 9 September 1971. In 1972

The British Army set up 321 Explosive Ordnance Disposal Company to tackle IRA bombs. The unit pioneered IED disposal, responding to over 54,000 emergency calls during the Troubles. There have been over 19,000 explosions and incendiary attacks. ATOs disposed of over 50 tons of explosives in another 6,300 incidents. (IWM HU 47328)

six EOD operators were killed in explosions, representing 50 per cent of the unit's operators killed during the Troubles.

While the IRA soon earned its reputation as a competent and sophisticated terrorist organization, this did not happen overnight. Indeed, in the early 1970s the IRA scored numerous 'own goals', whereby inexperienced and poorly trained bomb-makers blew themselves up while constructing, transporting and planting bombs. For instance, in February 1972 two Republicans, Patrick Casey and Eamonn Gamble, blew themselves up while tinkering with a bomb at temporary council offices in a school hall in Keady. Two IRA men, aged 19 and 20, were killed when the bomb they were transporting exploded prematurely, leaving their vehicle in a tangled mess in King Street, Magherafelt. In Crumlin, near Lough Neagh, two IRA volunteers died when the bomb they were transporting by barge exploded, killing both of them instantly. Four IRA men died when the bomb they were transporting along the Knockbreda Road went off, obliterating their car.

A bomb explodes in the centre of Belfast. Bombings of commercial targets became commonplace as the IRA's campaign intensified in the early 1970s. (Fred Hoare)

On 9 March 1972 four members of the IRA's 2nd Belfast Battalion working with explosives in a house on the Falls Road met a swift end when they crossed a wrong wire. On 7 April three other IRA men (all aged 17) died when they blew themselves up in Bawnmore Park in North Belfast. A devastating premature explosion on 28 May claimed the lives of a further four IRA volunteers and four civilians, highlighting the dangers of working in enclosed residential surroundings. Three more IRA men met a similar fate at the beginning of August, as did three of their comrades and six innocent civilians, when a premature explosion ripped through the customs office at Newry. Thirteen more IRA men and six others were to die in similar incidents before the end of the year. These 'own goals' highlighted the inherent danger of using the bomb as a lethal weapon in close proximity to the civilian population.

The year 1972 was the worst year for the Troubles. In total the IRA carried out 1,200 operations that year, mainly in rural areas of the province. Yet it also planted many large car bombs in the centre of Belfast in a bid to make Northern Ireland unstable and thereby, in the IRA's eyes, hasten the departure of the British state. Six Protestants

and one Catholic died when the IRA exploded a car bomb in Donegall Street, Belfast, on 20 March 1972. An inadequate warning had been given by the IRA. In July 1972 the IRA exploded three no-warning car bombs in Claudy, not far from Derry/Londonderry City, killing nine people, including a child. The bombing itself provoked massive outrage, particularly because it now appeared that the IRA was carrying out reprisals against civilians.

With an upsurge in violent attacks the British government sought alternative ways to deal with the IRA's bombing campaign. In early July 1972 an IRA delegation, including Gerry Adams, who was on remand in the cages of Long Kesh prison camp, and Martin McGuinness, was flown to London for a secret meeting with William Whitelaw, the Secretary of State for Northern Ireland. The talks amounted to little and the truce declared by the IRA was terminated against the backdrop of a renewed IRA offensive. While the clumsy 'own goals' were removing many bomb-makers from IRA ranks, the casualties did not lessen the determination of the organization to strike at the heart of the Protestant community more directly. On 21 July 1972 the IRA exploded 22 no-warning car bombs across Belfast in a blitz that saw six soldiers, two civilians and a UDA activist die and over 130 injured within an area with a one-mile radius. The Security Forces struggled to contain the violence.

Against the increasingly indiscriminate nature of paramilitary violence, the Ministry of Defence issued a more comprehensive set of Rules of Engagement (ROE) for soldiers in Northern Ireland. Known more commonly as the 'yellow card', these new ROE gave troops the option to return fire if their lives were threatened (i.e. for self-defence purposes) and as long as, in their own judgement, they believed there to be a threat. As the ROE explained: 'Soldiers may fire without warning if there is no other way to protect themselves or those whom it is their duty to protect from the danger of being killed or seriously injured.' Owing to the high intensity of gun and bomb attacks, the ROE also authorized troops to use heavy weapons under certain circumstances:

... a company commander may order the firing of heavy weapons (such as the Carl Gustav [a recoilless rifle]) against positions from which there is sustained hostile firing, if he believes that this is necessary for the preservation of the lives of soldiers or of other persons whom it is his duty to protect. In deciding whether or not to use heavy weapons full account must be taken of the risk that the opening of fire may endanger the lives of innocent persons.

Interestingly, the ROE detailed here had already been tightened up in the wake of the Bloody Sunday shootings. What these ROE overlooked was the procedure to be used in the treatment of terrorist suspects. The Compton Committee was later commissioned to investigate whether some detainees had been subjected to inhuman and degrading treatment. Compton found that while there had been physical ill-treatment, such as the application of the so-called five techniques used previously in Aden, there was insufficient evidence of brutality.

Nevertheless, the increase in shootings and bombings left the British government with a dilemma. There was immense public pressure to do something to tackle the IRA's campaign of violence and to ensure that the Stormont government's writ ran throughout the province. A Top Secret Cabinet Conclusion indicated London's thinking at the time:

The anger of the Protestant community had been such that, if he [the Prime Minister] and the Secretary of State for Defence had not immediately authorised sterner measures by the security forces against the IRA, there would have been a very serious risk of direct action on the streets on a widespread scale. The operations that had been undertaken had done much to calm Protestant opinion; nevertheless they had made no more than modest inroads upon the operational capability of the IRA, and had predictably caused some alienation of Roman Catholic opinion.

It was decided in London that the Army's Operation *Motorman* would be given the

The aftermath of a no-warning car bomb in Donegall Street, Belfast, on 20 March 1972. Seven people were killed and 150 injured in the explosion. It was typical of the type of attacks perpetrated by terrorists on all sides during the conflict. (Fred Hoare)

'Bloody Friday', Belfast, 21 July 1972

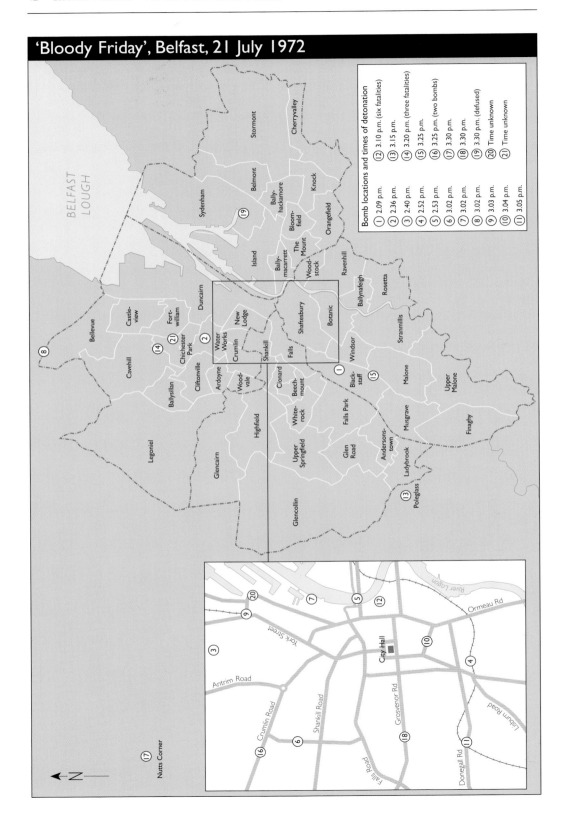

Bomb locations and times of detonation

① 2.09 p.m.
② 2.36 p.m.
③ 2.40 p.m.
④ 2.52 p.m.
⑤ 2.53 p.m.
⑥ 3.02 p.m.
⑦ 3.02 p.m.
⑧ 3.02 p.m.
⑨ 3.03 p.m.
⑩ 3.04 p.m.
⑪ 3.05 p.m.
⑫ 3.10 p.m. (six fatalities)
⑬ 3.15 p.m.
⑭ 3.20 p.m. (three fatalities)
⑮ 3.25 p.m.
⑯ 3.25 p.m. (two bombs)
⑰ 3.30 p.m.
⑱ 3.30 p.m.
⑲ 3.30 p.m. (defused)
⑳ Time unknown
㉑ Time unknown

green light to retake no-go areas in Belfast and Derry/Londonderry.

In Derry/Londonderry 8 (Infantry) Brigade had at its disposal nine regular infantry battalions, two UDR battalions, two Royal Engineer field squadrons, a troop of four Centurion AVREs (Armoured Vehicles Royal Engineers, a version of the Centurion tank) and a further seven minor units. Under cover of darkness the units moved into position on 31 July 1972. At 0400 hours the operation was launched. The infantry battalions, closely supported by the Royal Engineers, moved quickly to dominate their Tactical Areas of Responsibility and remove the barricades. In a radio broadcast, William Whitelaw made clear the government's intention to restore law and order by any means necessary, thus ensuring that the IRA was given adequate warning of the impending military manoeuvres. As with many earlier head-on engagements, the IRA chose to retreat to their safe havens across the border. Only token resistance was met by the Army as Operation *Motorman* swung into

Lieutenant-Colonel John Mottram, Commanding Officer of 40 Commando, Royal Marines, talks to ITN after the removal of barricades in the New Lodge Road area of Belfast. Operation *Motorman* was launched on 31 July 1972 to retake 'no-go' areas in Belfast and Derry/Londonderry from the IRA. (IWM MH 30542)

action, but a civilian and an unarmed IRA member were killed. By now troops were saturating Belfast and Derry/Londonderry, taking all of their objectives by 0730 hours.

Although Operation *Motorman* inflicted a short-term defeat on the IRA in both cities, it did not make the organization any less dangerous in other parts of Northern Ireland. In an incident at Sanaghanroe near Dungannon at 2300 hours on 10 September 1972, three soldiers from 1st Battalion, The Argyll and Sutherland Highlanders, were killed and four injured when their Saracen armoured personnel carrier was blown up. All those killed were in their early twenties. The sheer force of the blast lifted the armoured vehicle off the ground and threw it 15–20 yards through a hedge and into a

Soldiers board a Lynx helicopter in South Armagh. The upsurge in the use of roadside bombs and IEDs constrained the Army's movement by road, thus making the ferrying of troops by air essential. (Author's collection)

field. The bomb attack left a crater 30ft in diameter and 12–15ft deep. In this incident the IRA's firing point was 70–80 yards away, up a hill within sight of the road. Two weeks later another bomb was detonated directly in front of a Saracen armoured vehicle, causing the same devastating result; remarkably, the two soldiers escaped with only minor injuries.

Republicans carried out over 35 IED attacks on the Army in August 1972 alone. As one confidential Army report from the time put it, 'The tactics of the IRA may change as a result of Op MOTORMAN and attacks on the Security Forces in the rural areas could increase; the increased use of command detonated mines is all too likely'. The command-detonated IED was the commonest weapon in the IRA's armoury and would become more sophisticated as the conflict progressed. Such bombs were typically constructed using 200–300lb (91–136kg) of explosive packed into a milk churn and placed under a culvert or dug into a grass verge at the side of a road. They were detonated by command wire and (later) remote-firing mechanisms, causing massive carnage. These devices had far-reaching effects on the military's movement on the

ground. In an interview with the author one soldier who survived an IRA attack described how it felt:

One night on patrol in County Londonderry we were travelling along in our vehicles and we heard a bang. We immediately assumed that it was a contact. Our Royal Engineer search adviser later came out and, after surveying the scene, informed us that it had been a 1,000lb [454kg] bomb, which had detonated as we passed over a culvert, narrowly missing us. We had a few lucky escapes.

The increasing sophistication and lethality of IRA mine strikes and IED attacks, particularly in rural areas, necessitated the development of electronic counter-measures (ECM). In an interview with the author one seasoned veteran of Operation *Banner* recalled how his life 'was saved on more than one occasion' by the 'ECM bubble'. As the Army's 'lessons-learned' pamphlet *Military Operations in Northern Ireland* makes clear, this 'situation rapidly evolved into a continuous struggle between development and counter'.

In response to the growing number of military casualties caused by roadside bombs, the MoD gave more careful consideration to the use of helicopters to ferry troops. In one threat assessment the Army concluded that the main tactical weapon in the IRA's armoury was its volunteers' ability to withdraw hastily after carrying out armed actions by exploiting their knowledge of the local terrain:

Terrorist tactics are normally based on hit-and-run techniques both on foot and in cars. Ambushes, whether from which to snipe or command-detonate a mine, are relatively easy to set up but depend for their success on the availability of a rapid method of withdrawal. Withdrawal routes are often over fields where the terrorist has too great a head start on Security Force pursuers, or along nearby roads which cannot be reached quickly enough by Security Force vehicles which are, in any case, unsuited to chase getaway cars.

Use of helicopters increased and was soon exploited for other ends too, particularly since the Gazelle model provided a continuously available airborne reconnaissance and surveillance platform.

There were practical advantages to using the helicopter as a troop transporter, which 2 Para's experience in South Armagh on their third emergency tour bears out. Deployed on 27 March 1973 to what Merlyn Rees later labelled 'bandit country', the battalion would lose four of their own men on Armagh's roads, plus two soldiers of 17th/21st Royal Lancers and a Royal Engineer Search Advisor. Private Steven Norris and Lance Corporal Terence Brown died when their Land Rover was blown up by a 300lb (137kg) mine hidden under a culvert in Tullyogallaghan on 7 April 1973. Another soldier serving with 2 Para at the time recalls how one of his abiding memories of the tour was the blood-soaked stretchers being washed down in the shower block at Bessbrook.

In another incident four weeks later Company Sergeant-Major Ron Vines of 2 Para was killed when a pressure-pad he stepped on initiated a landmine explosion. The device's command wire led across the border near Moybane, south-east of Crossmaglen. As Company Sergeant-Major Vines walked over to a roadside wall, the 400lb (181kg) IRA bomb detonated, killing him instantly. His wife later said that she 'didn't even have a body to bury'. In the follow-up operation mounted by the Army in the aftermath of the explosion two other soldiers, Troopers Terence Williams and John Gibbons of 17th/21st Royal Lancers, were blown up by a secondary device on the same spot where Company Sergeant-Major Vines had died. An Army spokesman later said that the mood of the local civilian population in South Armagh had been 'extremely hostile'. Support for the IRA was high in Republican areas. As one former IRA volunteer recalled while speaking to the author, 'you cannot run a guerrilla campaign without the support of the community'.

Known as 'the workhorse of the campaign', the Westland Wessex helicopter was in service with the RAF from the mid-1960s. It was withdrawn from Operation *Banner* in 2002. (Author's collection)

As the conflict progressed the Army became better at countering IRA anti-personnel devices. The implementation of a rigorous pre-deployment training package delivered by the Northern Ireland Training Team (NITAT) to all units in the United Kingdom and Germany served to hone the Army's tactical skills and drills. In an interview with the author, one former UDR officer who served on the Directing Staff at NITAT in Sennelager, Germany, said that troops were put through rigorous training so that when they arrived 'in theatre' for operations, 'the more you could plant those wee seeds the better they were prepared'. Debriefs were especially important because soldiers soon became accustomed to the intelligence picture and how their role was vital in the overall security situation. When they eventually deployed to the province, units underwent further training in counter-IED tactics, advanced search techniques, and the application of ROE.[2]

---

2   In order to counter 'skills fade' the Army also introduced 'roulement' battalions that would deploy for pre-defined periods of time of several months in high-intensity areas, such as West Belfast, and 'resident' battalions that would move their headquarters and sub-units to Northern Ireland with their families for longer tours of up to two years.

Police primacy

By the mid-1970s the Labour government in London was exploring possible exit strategies from the conflict. London was beginning to place a premium on bolstering the profile of the RUC and the locally recruited UDR, the British Army's youngest and by now its largest infantry regiment, under a policy of 'Ulsterization'. This policy of handing over responsibility for security matters to local indigenous security forces had characterized Britain's approach to counter-insurgency and counter-terrorist operations throughout the post-war period. During the Mau Mau Emergency in Kenya in the 1950s Britain opted for 'Africanization', in which the colonial government backed up by British troops formed, equipped and trained 'Home Guard' units to protect vulnerable villages from attack. In the 1960s, during the Aden Emergency, British forces again mentored Federation troops under the guiding principle of 'Arabization', as Aden made the transition towards independence.

The UDR was the latest in a long line of what would today be called 'security transitions'. Established in 1970 as an instrument to counter terrorism in the province, the UDR was deemed to be invaluable because its members lived and worked in the areas where they soldiered and could thus draw on their excellent local knowledge. However, unlike the 'B' Specials, the UDR was born out of the political attempts to make military back-up more indigenous. While it was thought that the UDR would attract sufficient numbers of Catholics, this hope soon proved ill-founded for a variety of reasons, not least because the IRA intimidated many Catholics into leaving its ranks. Formed largely along British military lines, the UDR was fortunate to be able to call upon the professionalism of its Permanent Staff Instructors, many of whom had transferred into or were on attachment from the regular British Army regiments.

In setting up a ministerial committee to examine security policy in Northern Ireland Merlyn Rees, Secretary of State for Northern Ireland 1974–76, said that it should seek

... [t]o examine the action and resources required for the next few years to maintain law and order in Northern Ireland, including how best to achieve the primacy of the Police; the size and role of locally recruited forces; and the progressive reduction of the Army as soon as is practicable.

Rees made a significant impact on Northern Ireland politics. His approach to the problems dividing Northern Ireland's two communities tended to be 'theoretical, almost scholarly', according to the journalist Robert Fisk, and until the Ulster Workers Council (UWC) strike of May 1974, it seemed that Northern Ireland had 'acquired an enthusiastic, sensitive, highly intelligent minister who could combine political flexibility with toughness'. Nevertheless, the resilience of Loyalist workers, backed up by paramilitary muscle, left him politically wounded. Perhaps the most searing critique of Rees' handling of the UWC strike, from Fisk, was that '[h]e was trying to graft someone else's ideas onto someone else's government in someone else's country'. The strike effectively 'broke British policy in Ulster' and ensured that Protestant Unionists would not have 'power-sharing with an Irish dimension' thrust upon them. Rees bounced back from the debacle, later forging ahead with the Labour government's plan to place responsibility for security back into the hands of the RUC, thus laying the foundations for the successful evidence-based approach that would characterize Britain's commitment to countering Irish terrorism. The Army's role was dramatically scaled back in favour of raising the RUC's profile, with the assumption that the UDR would provide tactical assistance as and when required.

Northern Ireland was a unique soldiering environment. It demanded not only the confident application of infantry skills, such as proficiency in weapons-handling techniques and fieldcraft, but also a high level of Internal Security drills. The province's terrain was variable and ranged from the 303 miles of (largely rural) border separating north and south to the tight alleyways of inner-city Belfast. Peter Morton, formerly Commanding Officer 3 Para, explained how 'the fighting machine must be broken up into individuals and small teams who can think and operate sensitively, intelligently and always within the law no matter how provocative or frightening the situation they find themselves'.

The UDR soon became experts in the tactical side of the campaign and their numbers were increased as regular troops were withdrawn for duties elsewhere. Troop numbers rose steadily in the 1970s. At the time of Operation *Motorman* there were

approximately 19 units on the Army's Order of Battle in Northern Ireland, the equivalent of 21,000 troops. That figure declined to 15 units in 1975, to 13 in 1979, and again to nine in 1982. The number of troops stationed in the province in the 1980s levelled out at roughly 10,500.

The reduction in the numbers of regular troops, however, masked another important change in the operational tempo of the Army's role in Northern Ireland. In response to the nakedly sectarian murders of ten Protestant workmen near Kingsmill, South Armagh, on 5 January 1976, Prime Minister Harold Wilson authorized the deployment of the SAS to the area. Perhaps anticipating the steady build-up of pressure from Special Forces, the Provisional IRA took the decision

Table 3. Security Forces strength, 1969–98

Year	Regular	UDR/RIR	Army Total	RUC Total	Total
1969	2,700	0	2,700	3,500	6,200
1970	6,300	2,292	8,592	3,750	12,342
1971	7,800	4,044	11,844	4,083	15,927
1972	14,300	8,476	22,776	4,273	27,049
1973	16,900	8,443	25,343	4,421	29,764
1974	16,200	7,815	24,015	4,563	28,578
1975	15,000	7,692	22,692	4,902	27,594
1976	15,500	7,645	23,145	5,253	28,398
1977	14,300	7,651	21,951	5,692	27,643
1978	14,400	7,970	22,370	6,110	28,480
1979	13,600	7,518	21,118	6,614	27,732
1980	11,900	7,376	19,276	6,935	26,211
1981	11,600	7,470	19,070	7,334	26,404
1982	10,900	7,111	18,011	7,717	25,728
1983	10,200	6,925	17,125	8,003	25,128
1984	10,000	6,468	16,468	8,127	24,595
1985	9,700	6,494	16,194	8,259	24,453
1986	10,500	6,408	16,908	8,234	25,142
1987	11,400	6,531	17,931	8,236	26,167
1988	11,200	6,393	17,593	8,231	25,824
1989	11,200	6,230	17,430	8,259	25,689
1990	10,500	6,043	16,543	8,243	24,786
1991	10,500	6,276	16,776	8,222	24,998
1992	12,000	5,417	17,417	8,483	25,900
1993	13,000	5,412	18,412	8,470	26,882
1994	11,759	5,241	17,000	8,469	25,469
1995	12,019	5,170	17,189	8,499	25,688
1996	11,815	4,855	16,670	8,424	25,094
1997	12,477	4,757	17,234	8,430	25,664
1998	12,346	4,598	16,944	8,495	25,439

Members of the UDR patrol in the Clough/Ballykinlar area in August 1977. Situated along the picturesque County Down coast in the foothills of the Mourne Mountains, Ballykinlar was the largest military training establishment in Northern Ireland. (IWM MH 30552)

in November 1976 to restructure its organization along cellular lines and prepare for a 'long war'. These internal machinations led inevitably to a resurgent Republican threat, making a permanent downsizing of the British Army garrison in the province unlikely. Moreover, there is evidence to suggest that an upsurge in IRA attacks in West Belfast had taken the Army by surprise, a jolt that, as one intelligence report candidly revealed, 'must be seen as further evidence of our lack of tactical intelligence in West Belfast'. While good operational intelligence remained somewhat elusive in West Belfast, the military was having success in other areas.

Harold Wilson resigned in March 1976 and in a cabinet reshuffle, his successor as prime minister, James Callaghan, appointed a new secretary of state for Northern Ireland, Roy Mason (replacing Merlyn Rees). A Yorkshireman and former miner who had been a leading trade unionist, Mason had served as defence secretary before taking up his new post at the Northern Ireland Office (NIO). Mason was an staunch opponent of terrorism. He particularly disliked the Provisional IRA and under his stewardship would become an avid supporter of the Security Forces' attempts to disrupt the IRA campaign.

Unlike his predecessors, Mason took a hardline attitude towards violence and his tenure as Northern Ireland Secretary was marked by an increase in Special Forces operations. As Mason made clear in a public statement in May 1977, 'The number of special security forces such as the SAS had been substantially increased and this trend would continue'. In a letter to his successor at the Ministry of Defence, Fred Malley, Mason wrote:

We have been aware for some time of the tremendous and lasting boost for public morale which followed the posting of an SAS Squadron to South Armagh sixteen months ago. It says a great deal for the SAS Regiment's reputation for professional skill in the counter-terrorist role that ever since their arrival, there have been calls for their operations to be extended and their number increased.

Noting the success of the Army's role in the covert war in Northern Ireland, Mason asked Malley 'whether more could be done'

to ensure 'a better success rate' and 'to give extra credence to our claim that the Army's expertise in dealing with terrorists continues to grow'. Mason's correspondence with Malley on covert operations demonstrates the British government's understanding of the changing character of the terrorist threat. In Mason's words: '[T]he problem has ceased to be one of large confrontations with rioters and is one of identifying and tracing and finding evidence against small groups of terrorists'. To that end Mason became an enthusiastic supporter of the need for further covert action.

One of those serving in the ranks of the secret war was Captain Robert Nairac. A colourful if somewhat controversial figure, Nairac was a Liaison Officer between Special Forces and the RUC Special Branch. Someone who served with him told the author that Nairac 'had a great personality and made friends easily with the result that he was an

British Army brigade areas in the 1980s

excellent Liaison Officer'. On an undercover mission to meet a contact at the Three Steps pub in Drumintee, Nairac was beaten and abducted by the IRA. One of the IRA men who tortured and killed Nairac later admitted, 'I shot the British Captain. He never told us anything. He was a great soldier.' In February 1979 Nairac was posthumously awarded the George Cross, Britain's second-highest award for gallantry. Part of his citation read:

Captain Nairac served for four tours of duty in Northern Ireland totalling twenty-eight months. During the whole of this time he made an outstanding personal contribution: his quick analytical brain, resourcefulness, physical stamina and above all his courage and dedication inspired admiration in everyone who knew him.

As the Nairac case illustrates, the 'green Army' was not always privy to intelligence operations, which were undertaken on a 'need-to-know' basis. As General Sir Mike Jackson explained in his memoirs:

Intelligence and the response to it were handled on a very tight, need-to-know basis. Even when I was a brigade commander, I would not necessarily be in the loop. There would be a directive that uniformed troops were to keep out of a particular area between this time and that time because it had been 'sanitized' for a particular operation. I didn't always know what was going on, but I didn't always need to know.

With the intensification of the covert war in Northern Ireland the IRA was forced onto the back foot. Despite the odds now heavily stacked against it, though, the IRA remained resolute in its determination to drive the British Army from Northern Ireland. Speaking after his release from prison, former IRA Chief of Staff David O'Connell claimed that 'I am more personally

This photograph shows the scene of the booby-trap bomb explosion in October 1977 that killed Lieutenant Walter Kerr, a part-time member of the UDR. Republican terrorists used a sophisticated mercury tilt-switch mechanism attached to plastic explosives to kill and maim off-duty Security Forces personnel, thus necessitating routine under-car checks. (Courtesy of Pacemaker Press International)

Captain Robert Nairac GC was commissioned into the Grenadier Guards in 1972, serving four tours of Northern Ireland. He was abducted, tortured and shot by the IRA on 14 May 1977. His body has never been found. (Courtesy of the Sandhurst Collection)

convinced than ever of the validity of the basic strategy of calling for a declaration of intent'. For the IRA the only option open to the British government was to withdraw.

By May 1977 the Northern Ireland Office had other worries, with the anticipation of a second Loyalist industrial strike. The first, in 1974, had crippled Northern Ireland's infrastructure and led to the collapse of the power-sharing arrangement between Brian Faulkner's Unionist Party and Gerry Fitt's SDLP. This time, though, the Northern Ireland Office was ready for the strikers. In a secret memo sent by Mason to Callaghan, the former Defence Secretary noted:

If the strike takes place, the lesson of 1974 is that we need to display firmness and resolution from the start – and to make this clear in advance so that the action is expected. I am in close touch with the Chief Constable and the

GOC. Contingency plans are being updated. Knowledge that we are doing this will become apparent and will show that we mean business.

The widespread strike did not materialize, however. Intelligence made available to the British government suggested that the Revd Ian Paisley was 'now having cold feet about close involvement with the Loyalist paramilitaries'. Against this backdrop other intelligence reports suggested that 'the paramilitaries have worked themselves up into a state of considerable determination'. Nonetheless, in the words of one NIO official, after 36 hours of operations, the strike had 'scarcely caught the public imagination'.

Apart from industrial unrest from Loyalists the other major concern was the upsurge in killings by the Provisional IRA of members of the locally recruited UDR. In the late 1970s Republicans murdered over 50 members of the UDR. One killing was particularly shocking because it illustrated how members of the UDR were routinely targeted when they were off-duty. For the terrorists these 'soft targets' were much easier to eliminate because of the likelihood that they would be

This cache of IRA terrorist weapons was found during a search in Derry/Londonderry. These weapons included an M60 machine gun, three Armalite AR-15 rifles and a Star .357 Magnum pistol. Most were smuggled in by Republican supporters in the United States. (IWM HU 47343)

caught off-guard and unarmed. In other words, it fitted well with the IRA's decision to mitigate risk for its volunteers, despite propaganda that portrayed its volunteers as noble 'soldiers of Ireland'.

On 8 October 1977 Private Margaret Hearst, a part-time member of 2 UDR, was shot dead while sleeping in a caravan beside her parents' home near Middletown. Females had been admitted into the UDR from 1973 and it was Army policy for servicewomen to be unarmed, a stance that remained unchanged until the 1990s. A gunman broke into Hearst's parents' home, terrorized her aunt and two young brothers, and then entered the caravan in which she and her three-year-old daughter were sleeping. The 16-year-old IRA gunman fired ten or 11 shots at Private Hearst from an Armalite rifle, killing her instantly, but narrowly missing her young daughter. The gunman and his accomplices then fled the scene to the 'safe haven' of the Irish Republic, where they attended a dance in Monaghan. In the follow-up operation the murder weapon was uncovered in a hedgerow approximately 550 yards south of the Hearsts' home. Private Hearst was the first 'Greenfinch' (female member of the UDR) to be killed while off-duty; her murder, which was claimed by the IRA, was widely condemned.

Tragedy struck the Hearst family again in September 1980 when Private Hearst's father, Ross, was abducted and shot dead by the IRA. His 'crime', said the IRA, was to admit, during torture, that he had supplied information to the Security Forces. Not only was the organization targeting off-duty UDR soldiers, but it had now sunk to a new low by assassinating members of the wider Protestant community. Actions like these exposed the sectarian underbelly of Provisional IRA violence.

The IRA preferred to attack off-duty UDR personnel principally because their targets lived and worked in the communities they served, and were therefore vulnerable. UDR personnel – both full- and part-time – had to hide their profession for security reasons and entered into a routine of checking under cars and varying routes to and from their places of work and bases, as well as taking security measures to protect themselves and their families from attack. Of the 204 UDR and Royal Irish (Home Service Force) soldiers murdered, 162 (or 79 per cent) were killed off-duty, with some 60 ex-UDR members killed by Republicans.

In an interview with the author one former UDR soldier from the Derry/Londonderry area recalled how he 'ended up thinking like a terrorist in order to stay alive'. Opportunities for a social life were minimal, and the personal security precautions were such that one 'routinely had to check under your car for an under-car booby-trap bomb,' and 'vary routes to and from home and work'. One vignette sums up the atmosphere neatly:

I was followed home from work one night. I immediately realized that I was being followed. After speeding up to 94 miles per hour I slammed on the brakes. The hunter became the hunted. I followed suit but lost them. Running into a police checkpoint I then informed them of the car registration number. It later transpired that four prominent members of the IRA were out to kill me. They were dressed head-to-toe in khaki jackets.

Many UDR soldiers automatically assumed that IRA volunteers were out for a kill. The UDR soldier interviewed by the author recalled being asked on one occasion whether he would move home, to which he replied that they would track him down wherever he went – and, besides, had the IRA decided to attack his home, it was 'him or me': 'If they came to the house they would have found themselves in a battle' but they were 'fucking cowards'. In his words, 'the IRA never looked their victims in the eye ... except for the team led by [South Derry Republican Dominic McGlinchey] who made a point of doing that'.

Probing further, the murder campaign provoked strong feelings. The UDR soldier quoted above went on to say that 'I lost numerous friends. How did I feel? Anger

when a colleague was murdered. You wanted to seek revenge, but professionalism kicked in. Instinct kicked in and you got on with the job.' The same UDR man saw himself very much as 'the hunted'. The terrorists knew every move he made and he was engaged in a 'war of survival' on a daily basis. The primary weapon of the IRA on soft targets was an under-car booby-trap bomb. 'If you could counter their defences they observed you from a distance and a secondary attack – a shoot – was mounted.' The IRA, however, relied on the patterns set by Security Forces personnel, whether on or off-duty. 'Some journeys to and from work, such as a six-mile trip, which would take ten minutes in a normal society took half an hour. I wasn't driving directly to work and when I left work I never took the same route

The Queen's cousin, Lord Louis Mountbatten of Burma, pictured on his retirement in 1965, served as the last Viceroy of India in 1946–47 and Chief of the Defence Staff from 1959 to 1965. Lord Mountbatten was murdered on 27 August 1979, when his boat was blown up by the IRA. (IWM MH 28465)

This posthumous portrait shows Captain Herbert Westmacott MC, who served with the SAS in Northern Ireland. Commissioned into the Grenadier Guards, he was killed on 2 May 1980 by members of the IRA's infamous 'M60 gang' as he led his men in an arrest operation on the Antrim Road. (Courtesy of the Sandhurst Collection)

home.' Even so, the unpredictability of IRA attacks and the sophistication of their intelligence, targeting and killing capabilities made the IRA a versatile opponent.

Although the IRA had by now reorganized, Roy Mason warned that the group was now in possession of more sophisticated weapons and had successfully smuggled in at least one US-made M60 machine gun, which, he said, 'has probably been used'. Because of what he called 'their diminishing resources' Mason believed the IRA's aim was 'to find something different and the M60 is a new dimension'. Mason's comments came after off-duty UDR member, William Gordon, and his ten-year-old daughter Lesley were murdered by the IRA when an under-car booby-trap bomb blew up their family car outside their home in Maghera, County Derry/Londonderry, on

8 February 1978. His wife was waving goodbye with the couple's baby in her arms when the bomb exploded. The Gordons' seven-year-old son Richard, who was in the back seat at the time, was blown out of the car and onto the footpath. One eyewitness said that most of the car ended up on the roof of a house 60 yards away. Speaking in the wake of the attack and a few days after the La Mon Hotel atrocity, which claimed the lives of 12 Protestants, the Shadow Northern Ireland Secretary Airey Neave expressed the view that 'the Special Air Service on our side could play a big role here'. Within a year Neave was himself assassinated by the INLA when he was blown up as he drove out of the House of Commons car park.

The IRA successfully assassinated other high-profile targets too. On 27 August 1979 the organization murdered Lord Louis Mountbatten, the Queen's cousin, who was taking his pleasure boat out of the harbour at Mullaghmore, County Sligo, in the Irish Republic, when the IRA detonated a remote-control bomb. Lord Mountbatten's murder sent shockwaves through the British establishment. Two young boys, aged 14 and 15, one of them Lord Mountbatten's grandson, were also killed in the explosion. Civilians caught up in such attacks were regarded by the IRA and their apologists as 'collateral damage'. The murder of 18 soldiers in a co-ordinated attack later that day in Warrenpoint, County Down, demonstrated that the IRA could also execute bigger and more sophisticated operations.

The 'dirty war'

Attacks on the Security Forces became much more frequent in the early 1980s. The use of heavier-calibre weapons in the late 1970s alarmed government officials and military commanders. Special Forces were tasked with recovering arms caches and arresting IRA members. In one incident on 2 May 1980 an IRA ASU (Active Service Unit, the nomenclature adopted when the IRA

The Republican hunger strikes of 1981 were initiated as a means of extracting concessions from the authorities at the Maze Prison. The prison struggle gained support from many moderate nationalists. (Courtesy of Pacemaker Press International)

This mural in West Belfast depicts the hunger striker Bobby Sands. Sands became an IRA martyr when, aged 26, he died after refusing food for 66 days. (Aaron Edwards)

switched to a more tightly organized cellular unit structure) opened fire with an M60 on an eight-man SAS team as they stormed a house on the Antrim Road in North Belfast. The burst of fire killed the team leader, Captain Herbert Westmacott, instantly. The IRA unit had pre-planned the operation at a variety of different locations across the city, unaware of the presence of an informer in their ranks. Intelligence was passed on to the Task Co-ordinating Committee, the operational hub of the Security Forces based at HQNI in Lisburn, and the SAS were allocated the mission of neutralizing what became known as the 'M60 gang'. Owing to a map-reading error the SAS team entered the wrong house, with the terrorists holed up next door, a mistake which very nearly cost the lives of more soldiers.

Local New Lodge man Joe Doherty and another member of the ASU had been trained as snipers and knew the routine of Army patrols in the area well. The IRA's M60 gang had a fearsome reputation and was equipped with an assortment of other weapons, including a Heckler & Koch submachine gun and FAL self-loading rifles, as well as several handguns. Their gang's *modus operandi* had been to ambush Security Forces patrols as

they passed through Republican areas. The following year seven IRA men were charged with the SAS officer's murder, only for two of them to escape from custody.

The M60 was again used by the IRA on 16 July 1981, when 18 soldiers of 1st Battalion, The Royal Green Jackets (1 RGJ), on a four-month emergency tour were dropped off on a covert reconnaissance mission at Glassdrummond, between Crossmaglen and Forkhill. Within a matter of hours the close-observation platoon's position had been compromised by locals, who then alerted the IRA. Moments later an IRA ASU opened fire from across the border. The van used to extract the British soldiers was hit by 150 bullets from an assortment of weapons, including an M60, four Armalite rifles and a .303 rifle. Lance Corporal Gavin Dean was shot dead and two of his comrades wounded.

Only a few weeks before, on 19 May 1981, 1 RGJ had lost four riflemen and an attached driver from the Royal Corps of Transport in a massive landmine strike. Experts later said that a 1,000lb (454kg) bomb had totally obliterated the Saracen armoured car. Tragedy was not to end there for the regiment, however, as a roadside bomb claimed the lives of three more riflemen on 23 March

During the hunger strikes huge riots broke out across Northern Ireland. This photograph shows members of 2nd Battalion, The Royal Anglian Regiment, firing baton rounds at rioters in the Bogside, Derry/Londonderry, 1981. (IWM HU 41939)

1982, a couple of weeks into their residential tour. And in one of the most sickening attacks of the Troubles, two members of the Household Cavalry, the Queen's official bodyguard, were killed instantly when a car bomb exploded on the Mall, near Hyde Park in London. A second bomb placed under the bandstand was detonated simultaneously, claiming the lives of seven bandsmen of the Royal Green Jackets.

What made the mood of this period particularly intense was that military operations were conducted against the backdrop of a Republican hunger strike in the Maze prison over a dispute with the authorities. Eventually, ten IRA and INLA prisoners were to die, including Bobby Sands, who had been elected to Westminster as an MP for Fermanagh and South Tyrone.

Sands died on 5 May 1981 after refusing food for 66 days. Unsurprisingly, violence escalated in the wake of the hunger strikes. It led to a re-entrenchment of communities, and, interestingly, also to a groundswell in popular support for the dead Republicans, which in turn led to an improvement in Sinn Féin's electoral fortunes. The IRA increased its operations against the Army and in one particularly shocking incident five soldiers were blown up and killed in a mine-strike against their armoured personnel carrier near Omagh, County Tyrone.

Republican terrorists also returned to targeting off-duty soldiers. On 6 December 1982, a devastating no-warning bomb attack on the Droppin' Well pub in Ballykelly, close to Shackleton Barracks, killed 11 soldiers and six civilians. The INLA later admitted responsibility. Meanwhile, the IRA had renewed their campaign against the locally recruited UDR, abducting off-duty personnel before torturing and then shooting them. The fate of Sergeant Thomas Cochrane illustrates the ruthlessness and cold-blooded

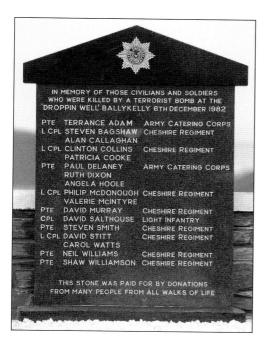

IN MEMORY OF THOSE CIVILIANS AND SOLDIERS
WHO WERE KILLED BY A TERRORIST BOMB AT THE
'DROPPIN' WELL' BALLYKELLY 6TH DECEMBER 1982

PTE	TERRANCE ADAM	ARMY CATERING CORPS
L CPL	STEVEN BAGSHAW	CHESHIRE REGIMENT
	ALAN CALLAGHAN	
L CPL	CLINTON COLLINS	CHESHIRE REGIMENT
	PATRICIA COOKE	
PTE	PAUL DELANEY	ARMY CATERING CORPS
	RUTH DIXON	
	ANGELA HOOLE	
L CPL	PHILIP McDONOUGH	CHESHIRE REGIMENT
	VALERIE McINTYRE	
PTE	DAVID MURRAY	CHESHIRE REGIMENT
CPL	DAVID SALTHOUSE	LIGHT INFANTRY
PTE	STEVEN SMITH	CHESHIRE REGIMENT
L CPL	DAVID STITT	CHESHIRE REGIMENT
	CAROL WATTS	
PTE	NEIL WILLIAMS	CHESHIRE REGIMENT
PTE	SHAW WILLIAMSON	CHESHIRE REGIMENT

THIS STONE WAS PAID FOR BY DONATIONS
FROM MANY PEOPLE FROM ALL WALKS OF LIFE

This memorial commemorates those murdered by the INLA at the Droppin' Well pub in Ballykelly on 6 December 1982. The bomb ripped through a packed nightclub bar, killing 17 people instantly. It was one of the worst atrocities in the Troubles. (IWM HU 98370)

nature of IRA violence against UDR members. On 17 October 1982, Cochrane was travelling home from his civilian job at Glennane linen mill near Markethill, South Armagh, when IRA members felled him from his motorcycle, bundled him into a car and took him away to where he was tortured. The organization released a statement saying he was being held for 'interrogation because of his crimes against the Nationalist community'. The IRA hoped to gain valuable intelligence about his comrades in the UDR; knowing that he was going to be killed, however, Cochrane gave his captors nothing. The IRA murdered him and dumped his body in Lislea, Armagh, five days after his abduction, proving yet again, in Ed Moloney's words, that 'targeting members of the ... [UDR] for death was an integral part of IRA strategy'.

In conversations with the author one former UDR member said that using predictable routes unfortunately left off-duty soldiers open to attack from terrorists. Speaking generally about the IRA's methods, he said, 'When they were kidnapped they were taken to killing houses where they were beaten and horrifically mutilated... That is the reality. And a bomb was placed under the body for Security Forces personnel as a "come on".'

One example of a 'come on' was the cold-blooded murder of a 62-year-old civilian chief instructor employed at Magilligan Prison. Leslie Jarvis, who attended night classes at Magee College, was shot dead as he sat in his car outside the college on 23 March 1987. His body was then booby-trapped and left for unsuspecting members of the Security Forces; the device exploded a short time later, killing two policemen who were investigating the shooting.

In a bid to reduce the IRA's capacity for mounting attacks on Security Forces personnel, the cutting edge of the Army's Special Forces units increasingly came to the forefront in the 1980s. As Mark Urban has observed, 'Throughout the ten years which followed [from 1976], the importance of the "Green Army" – groups of uniformed regular soldiers – in confronting terrorism fell as the role of undercover forces grew.' The undercover war was now overtaking the overt military presence as the SAS, Military Intelligence and other security agencies intensified their covert operations against Republican and Loyalist terrorists. In statistical terms, over 30 Provisional IRA members and two INLA members had been killed and many more arrested by undercover soldiers between 1976 and 1987. Some journalists have claimed that this high attrition rate was made possible only because Security Forces intelligence 'had been excellent'. Intelligence-gathering was the lifeblood of Security Forces operations throughout Operation Banner. One former undercover soldier told the author that 'the covert war was a bigger battle than the overt war'.

Perhaps one of the most controversial aspects of the Security Forces' secret war against the IRA and Loyalist paramilitaries was their ability to penetrate terrorist

The Loughgall Ambush, 8 May 1987

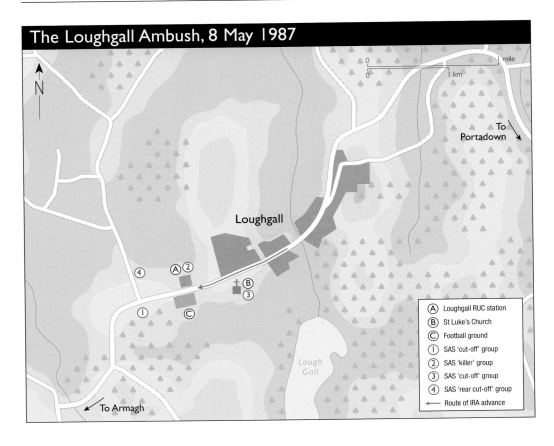

To Portadown

Loughgall

Lough Gall

To Armagh

(A) Loughgall RUC station
(B) St Luke's Church
(C) Football ground
(1) SAS 'cut-off' group
(2) SAS 'killer' group
(3) SAS 'cut-off' group
(4) SAS 'rear cut-off' group
← Route of IRA advance

The SAS operation at Loughgall on 8 May 1987 resulted in the deaths of eight members of the Provisional IRA. Five gunmen in this Toyota van, accompanied by a bomb-laden mechanical digger, were ambushed while attacking the village's RUC station. The PIRA Active Service Unit had attacked several Security Forces bases by driving into them with 500lb bombs hidden in the buckets of diggers. (Courtesy of Pacemaker Press International)

organizations with Human Intelligence sources, or agents. The number of these agents, known more commonly in paramilitary circles as 'touts', is difficult to quantify. That said, the Provisional IRA is said to have killed 70 suspected informers during their long campaign. In his book *The Secret History of the IRA*, Ed Moloney alleged that informers were responsible for compromising several of the IRA's missions in the late 1980s. Moloney claims that the unit most affected by informants was the Tyrone IRA, which had killed several hundred people during the Troubles, although had itself lost a total of 53 volunteers, of whom just over half – 28 – were killed in the five years after 1987.

On 8 May 1987 eight men from the Provisional IRA's East Tyrone Brigade were cut down in a hail of SAS bullets as they attempted to attack an RUC station in the sleepy County Armagh village of Loughgall.

A 24-strong SAS team had been assembled in Mahon Road Barracks, Portadown, on the evening before the shooting. Outnumbering the IRA by three to one they split up into a 'killer group' and three 'cut-off groups', each taking up position. The IRA had earlier hijacked a mechanical digger; loading a 200lb (91kg) bomb into its bucket, three of the terrorists travelled in its cab and five others in the blue Toyota HiAce van. The van reached Loughgall at 1915 hours, passing the church and driving down the hill to the station before going back up. After making sure the coast was clear it returned, closely followed by the mechanical digger. At about 1920 hours the van came to a halt in front of the station. The IRA men in the van dismounted and opened fire with their automatic weapons. At the same time the digger crashed into the wall and the IRA men on board lit the fuse, at which point the SAS ambush was sprung. Over 1,500 rounds were fired by the SAS soldiers and the elite policemen who were accompanying them.

This was not the first time the IRA had attacked RUC stations. On 28 February 1985 the IRA had mortared Newry RUC station, killing nine police officers, the largest single loss of life incurred by the RUC in the Troubles. In May that year the IRA blew up a mobile police patrol, killing four officers, and on 7 December they launched an attack on Ballygawley RUC barracks, killing two policemen. This last attack was much more audacious and involved IRA volunteers raking the police station with gunfire and then blowing it up. It was a tactic repeated again on 11 August 1986, when the IRA destroyed the RUC station at the Birches, County Tyrone.

In an oration at the graveside of the dead men, Gerry Adams said that Loughgall would become 'a tombstone for British policy in Ireland and a bloody milestone in the struggle for freedom, justice and peace'. Strategically, though, the IRA was staring defeat in the face. In the 1980s and 1990s nine out of every ten operations were aborted or failed. By now Security Forces intelligence operations were scoring huge successes.

Loyalist gunman Michael Stone moves away along the fence line after attacking the funeral of the IRA terrorists killed by the SAS in Gibraltar in March 1988. Stone murdered three IRA volunteers on the day. (Fred Hoare)

This photograph captures the moment when Corporals Derek Wood and David Howes were set upon by a Republican mob. They had strayed into the path of the funeral cortège and were abducted and shot by the Provisional IRA. The mourners believed they were Loyalists attempting to attack the funeral. (Courtesy of Pacemaker Press International)

Meanwhile, Loyalist violence reached a peak by the late 1980s and early 1990s. In part this was attributable to a more honed intelligence-gathering capability and an influx of new weaponry, which permitted the UVF and UDA to enhance the sophistication of their operations. Michael Stone's attack on the 'Gibraltar Three' funerals and the resulting IRA shooting of two off-duty British Army corporals reinforced the cycle of violence at this time. However, the shift from a random sectarian campaign of violence to a more focused and co-ordinated effort to assassinate individual Republicans led some Unionist politicians to suggest that the Loyalists were having an effect on the IRA. Nationalist politicians offered another reason for the successes of Loyalist paramilitaries: collusion.

Countless informants were recruited by the Security Forces, many of whom, it was alleged, took an active part in criminal acts such as extortion, intimidation and murder. It is thought that in a bid to root out informers in its ranks the IRA killed over 70 of its own volunteers. In response to allegations of collusion between some elements of the Security Forces and terrorist groups, Margaret Thatcher's Conservative

government appointed Sir John Stephens, the former Metropolitan Police Commissioner, to undertake an investigation into the UFF murders of a Catholic, Patrick Finucane, and a Protestant, Brian Adam Lambert. But so protracted was the process that his findings and recommendations for the period 1987–2003 were published only in April 2003. Towards the end of his report, Stephens concluded that

... there was collusion in both murders and the circumstances surrounding them. Collusion is evidenced in many ways. This ranges from the wilful failure to keep records, the absence of accountability, the withholding of intelligence and evidence, through to the extreme of agents being involved in murder.

Controversy still surrounds these killings and other incidents in the 'dirty war' and continues to dominate Republican thinking on the legacy of the Troubles.

Between 1987 and 1989 the RUC dealt with over 3,000 terrorist-related incidents, of which 261 were Troubles-related deaths. The Provisional IRA had by now been developing more deadly techniques. On 24 October

A proxy bomb attack on the Victor Two checkpoint on the Buncrana Road, Derry/Londonderry, on 24 October 1990 killed five soldiers and a civilian, 'Patsy' Gillespie. Gillespie's family were held at gunpoint by the IRA and he was forced to drive a van bomb into the Army base. (Courtesy of Pacemaker Press International)

A soldier examines an IRA mortar that has been rigged to the bucket of a mechanical digger. IRA bomb-makers were masters of the 'flying bomb' and frequently constructed home-made mortars. This mortar was abandoned in an aborted attack on the Security Forces in Bessbrook in the late 1980s. (IWM CT 629)

1990 it unveiled a deadly new tactic, when it carried out a 1,000lb (454kg) proxy bomb attack on the Coshquin PVCP (Permanent Vehicle Check Point).[3] Five soldiers from 1st Battalion, The King's Regiment, and a civilian (the driver of the van carrying the bomb) were killed. The civilian, Patrick 'Patsy' Gillespie, had worked in the canteen of a local Security Forces base. His family was taken hostage and held at gunpoint, while he was ordered to drive the van and its deadly cargo to the target.

The move towards Ulsterization since the mid-1970s was becoming a reality by the early 1990s. The UDR was a much more professional and adept organization. As one former UDR officer recalled in conversations with the author, 'the UDR grew from being a part-time, bunch of colonials into a more professional organization'. It had by now been given further operational responsibilities as the numbers of regular troops began to drop off, particularly as there were now pressures coming from the 1990 'Options for Change' defence review and overseas commitments in the Gulf. In the defence review a number of infantry regiments were amalgamated, including the UDR and the Royal Irish Rangers, leading to the formation of the Royal Irish Regiment in 1992.

The political and military pressure exerted on the IRA forced the organization to switch its attention to more high-profile targets on the British mainland. In February 1991 the IRA launched an audacious mortar attack on No. 10 Downing Street. A series of co-ordinated attacks on the London Stock Exchange applied further pressure, leading

---

3   PVCPs gave troops the flexibility to mount a permanent presence around their patrol bases and observation posts dotted along the border. Many of the Army's border bases were 'supersangars', 65ft-high watchtowers erected as surveillance and listening posts.

Unionist politician Robert McCartney to remark that 'a bomb in London is worth 100 in Belfast'. These attacks demonstrated how the IRA's campaign was increasing in intensity. A shipment of arms destined for Belfast was intercepted in 1994; however, there were suggestions that more than three-quarters of the consignment had successfully reached its destination.

While there was a dip in the number of operations mounted by the IRA, Loyalist violence continued unabated. The brutal sectarian killings of four workmen in Castlerock on 25 March 1993 and the indiscriminate attack on the Rising Sun bar in Greysteel, near Derry/Londonderry City, on 30 October that year were particularly shocking. The Greysteel massacre was exceptionally callous, with UFF gunman Torrens Knight and his accomplice heard shouting 'trick or treat' before opening fire, spraying the packed bar with over 30 bullets. There were 200 people in the bar that evening; it was a miracle that the attack claimed only eight victims. The Greysteel

A British soldier stands guard outside shops in the Shankill Road just after the outbreak of a feud between Loyalists in August 2000. The violence led to seven deaths, several injuries and hundreds of families having to move home. (IWM HU 98346)

attack was mounted in retaliation for the IRA bombing of Frizzel's fish-and-chip shop on the Shankill Road a few days earlier, which claimed the lives of nine civilians. The IRA volunteer responsible, Thomas Begley, also died as the bomb he was transporting blew up prematurely. Issuing a statement to the media shortly afterwards, the IRA claimed that the operation was intended to target a meeting of the UFF in an upstairs office. Violence continued steadily into 1994, as the IRA targeted Heathrow Airport on three separate occasions in March that year. Meanwhile it also undertook a co-ordinated assassination campaign in which a number of high-profile Loyalists were shot dead. On all fronts the violence continued unchecked with little prospect of an end in sight.

Soldiering the peace: General Sir Mike Jackson GCB, CBE, DSO, DL

General Sir Mike Jackson has held every rank in the British Army from officer cadet to general. Born in 1944, he attended the Royal Military Academy Sandhurst in 1962–63; commissioned into the Intelligence Corps, he later transferred into the Parachute Regiment. Jackson served three tours of Northern Ireland. In the first, from 1970, as a captain, he was a Community Relations Officer/Unit Press Officer and later, from the spring/summer of 1971 until 1972, as a major, Adjutant of 1 Para, based at Palace Barracks; in the second, between January 1979 and December 1980, he was Officer Commanding B Company, 2 Para; in the third, between November 1989 and Easter 1992, he was Commander of 39 (Infantry) Brigade in Lisburn.

Jackson witnessed first-hand how the tempo of the Army's military operations changed over time, from its early peacekeeping role in 1970, through to its counter-insurgency drive against the Provisional IRA, and finally into its counter-terrorist phase. Later reflecting on his service in Northern Ireland, he said he was 'a round peg in a round hole'.

In 1970 1 Para was the reserve battalion for 39 Brigade. Jackson was Community Relations Officer/Unit Press Officer. He later remarked in his autobiography that he found this role 'very stimulating' and 'relished the challenge – not least because the job took me out on to the streets wherever there was trouble'. The 39 Brigade commander at that time was Frank Kitson, who had just completed a Defence Fellowship at Oxford and published an influential book, *Low Intensity Operations*. Jackson said of Kitson that although he was not the most senior officer in Northern Ireland at that time, he was 'the sun around which the planets revolved, and he very much set the tone for

the operational style'. Kitson's command appointment coincided with the IRA's decision to begin offensive operations against the British Army.

A ruthless and determined guerrilla enemy in the form of the IRA faced the Security Forces in the early 1970s. One of its most deadly units was the Derry Brigade, at one time led by Martin McGuinness (later Deputy First Minister), which murdered over 200 people between 1970 and 1994. Since the souring of relations between the Army and the Catholic community in 1970–71, the IRA began to target and attack Security Forces personnel more directly.

The intensity of IRA attacks had been increasing markedly in the opening weeks of 1972. On 27 January, as they travelled in an unmarked car up the steep incline of Creggan Hill towards Rosemount RUC station, Sergeant Peter Gilgunn, 26, and Constable David Montgomery, 20, were shot dead, and their colleague Constable Charlie Maloney was badly wounded. The IRA gunmen responsible stepped out in front of their car and sprayed their Ford Cortina with automatic fire from a Thompson submachine gun, hitting it 17 times. Gilgunn and Montgomery were the first RUC officers to be murdered in the city for 50 years and the latest of 18 policemen to be killed by Republicans since 1969.

Interestingly, on the same day as this attack, the British Army fought a major gun-battle with an IRA unit led by Martin Meehan in Dungooley, South Armagh, during which a detachment of the Royal Scots Dragoon Guards fired over 4,500 rounds of ammunition. The IRA responded in kind, firing assault rifles and an anti-tank weapon at the troops. In response to the upsurge in violence, Defence Secretary Lord Carrington imposed constraints on the

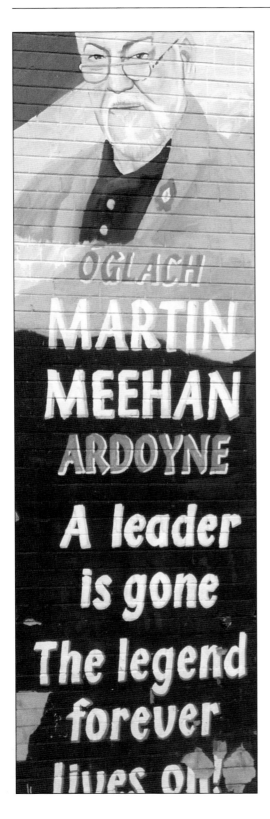

A mural depicting Provisional IRA gunman Martin Meehan, who led several attacks against British troops from the 1970s onwards. (Aaron Edwards)

Army operating in Derry/Londonderry. On a visit to the city on 7 January 1972, Commander Land Forces (Northern Ireland) Major-General Robert C. Ford reported how 'the Army in Londonderry is for the moment virtually incapable' and that the minimum-force policy was failing to allow the troops to restore law and order. As he continued, 'I am coming to the conclusion that the minimum force necessary to achieve a restoration of law and order is to shoot selected ring leaders amongst the DYH [Derry Young Hooligans]'.

At 1610 hours on 30 January 1972, Jackson witnessed the Paras entering the Bogside. He later told the Saville Inquiry that '[I]t became almost immediately apparent that they had become involved in a firefight'. Moving forwards with his commanding officer, Derek Wilford, to get a better view of what was happening, he recalled, '[a]s I sprinted across the wasteground I had an absolutely firm impression that I was being shot at. What I thought was: "some bugger is firing at me".' Within 30 minutes 108 shots had been fired and 13 people lay dead, with another 14 injured. Soldiers manning a machine-gun post had earlier fired the shots that wounded John Johnson, who later died of his wounds.

Bloody Sunday was a tragedy for the people of Derry/Londonderry. It was a major catalyst in the further deterioration of relations between the Army and the sections of the Catholic minority who had not yet turned against them. The shootings unleashed a tidal wave of support around the world for nationalists and Republicans. On 2 February 1972, the British Embassy in Dublin was overrun and burned down by an angry mob. Meanwhile, the IRA enjoyed a recruiting bonanza, as 'the stench of cordite was clearing from Rossville Street', in Eamonn McCann's words. Young men flocked to the IRA's banner with one thing in mind: to hit back.

Soon the IRA was seeking reprisals against civilians. An upsurge in its bombing campaign reduced much of Derry/Londonderry to rubble, sending a clear signal to Unionists that they were unwanted and that 'Free Derry' had become a 'no-go' area. In Belfast the IRA exploded 22 no-warning bombs inside a one-mile radius in 75 minutes, killing nine people and injuring over 120; the day became known as 'Bloody Friday'. In response the British government authorized Operation *Motorman*, a retaking of no-go areas. However, on the same day, and as a means of relieving pressure on its volunteers, the IRA detonated three no-warning car-bombs in the town of Claudy, just a few miles outside the city, killing nine people and injuring scores more. The year 1972 was the single worst year of the Troubles, with a total of 497 people killed.

The IRA carried out over 1,200 operations in 1972, mainly in rural areas. Early military intelligence reports suggested that Republicans would

… extend guerrilla warfare to rural areas of south Co. Londonderry. Hideouts and arms dumps are being constructed for this purpose. Active Service Units from Eire together with local units are expected to take part in hit and run attacks against Security Forces, and it is hoped that some of the Roman Catholic rural areas will become No-Go areas.

Violence against the Security Forces escalated in the period after the shootings in Derry/Londonderry. A total of 14 RUC officers and 53 soldiers lost their lives in the two-and-a-half years before 30 January 1972, while 26 RUC officers and 180 soldiers were murdered in the two-and-a-half years after 'Bloody Sunday'. A startling 130 troops died in 1972 alone.

This was certainly the atmosphere Jackson left behind when he departed several months later; it remained virtually unchanged when he returned for his second tour in January 1979. He had assumed command of B Company, 2 Para, who were based in South Armagh and acted as the reserve battalion for 3 (Infantry) Brigade. Jackson had just

returned from operations with his company to the headquarters of 1st Battalion, The Queen's Own Highlanders (1 QOH), in Bessbrook Mill, South Armagh, when A Company was tasked with relieving 2 Para's Support Company in Newry. On Bank Holiday Monday, 27 August 1979, A Company set off on a random route selected from a number of possible routes provided by the operations (ops) room in Ballykinlar. As Jackson noted in his memoirs, it was a course of action that was 'to result in mayhem', for the IRA had laid a meticulously planned ambush.

The first bomb, constructed with half a ton of explosives, was disguised beneath hay on the back of a flatbed lorry. The IRA detonated it by remote control as the three-vehicle convoy passed by, killing six Paras in the rear four-ton truck instantly. Those in the lead two vehicles, a Land Rover and another four-tonner, debussed to cordon off the area and help their wounded comrades. Almost immediately news filtered into the ops room at Bessbrook, where Jackson was enjoying a cup of tea in the officers' mess. A report had come in from a nearby Royal Marines patrol that an explosion had occurred on the main road from Warrenpoint to Newry at 1640 hours. A Wessex helicopter returning from a routine mission intercepted the frantic contact message radioed by the soldiers. The crew quickly relayed it back to Bessbrook and were ordered to return and pick up a medical team and four-man quick reaction force.

The helicopter arrived at the scene to ferry away the wounded. Just as it took off – 20 minutes after the initial explosion – a second bomb, about 200 yards further along the road towards Newry, was detonated by the IRA, killing 12 more soldiers who were taking cover by a gate lodge nearly. The second explosion claimed the life of one of the highest-ranking officers to be killed in the Troubles, Lieutenant-Colonel David Blair of 1 QOH. Blair was airborne in a Gazelle helicopter when he received word of the explosion and ordered the pilot to land close to the scene. He was dropped off, together with his signaller, in the grounds of a country house, from where they ran down to the gate lodge. At this point the terrorists, who had been watching events unfold, detonated the second bomb. Eyewitnesses reported hearing heavy automatic gunfire from the Irish Republic, across the narrow canal.

Jackson recalled in his memoirs how '[a]s we circled before landing I could see two craters and large scorch-marks on the road marking where the bombs had been'. The scene that greeted him when he landed was horrifying. Soldiers lay screaming; 'there was human debris everywhere', he said, 'mostly unidentifiable lumps of red flesh, but among them torsos, limbs, heads, hands and ears'. The Warrenpoint massacre had a profound effect on the future Chief of the General Staff. 'I still have ugly pictures in my head from that terrible day. Once you've seen such appalling sights you can't close your mind to them. But I don't have nightmares;

fortunately my temperament isn't like that,' he wrote. It was the biggest loss for the Paras since Arnhem in 1944.

When the Gulf War broke out Jackson was commanding 39 (Infantry) Brigade in Belfast; it was the second time that he was to miss out on combat, having been posted to a Defence Intelligence-gathering post in MoD Main Building during the Falklands War of 1982. He wrote that in 'some ways not much had changed since my last tour'. Although there was much less mass rioting, 'appalling atrocities' continued. Just as he arrived he got a report of a roadside bomb that had killed three members of 3 Para in Mayobridge, County Down.

Jackson's job as brigadier was 'to task, to co-ordinate, to encourage and to support the soldiers: to ensure that everybody knew what they were supposed to be doing, and that they had the resources they needed, including reinforcements if necessary'. In short he

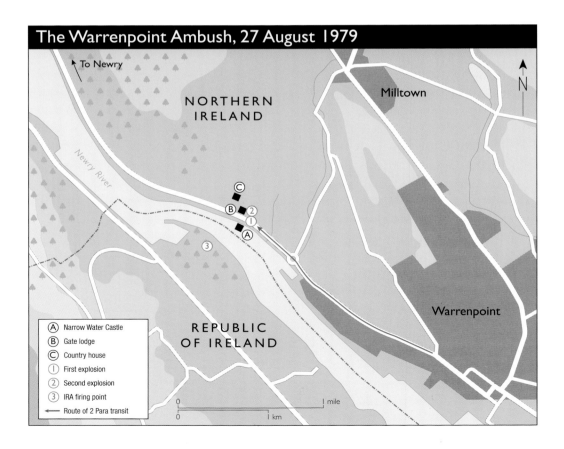

The Warrenpoint Ambush, 27 August 1979

To Newry

NORTHERN IRELAND

Milltown

N

Newry River

Warrenpoint

REPUBLIC OF IRELAND

Ⓐ Narrow Water Castle
Ⓑ Gate lodge
Ⓒ Country house
① First explosion
② Second explosion
③ IRA firing point
⟵ Route of 2 Para transit

0   1 mile
0   1 km

The then-Chief of the General Staff, Sir Mike Jackson, talks to HRH Prince William after HRH Prince Harry's commissioning at the Sovereign's Parade at the Royal Military Academy Sandhurst on 12 April 2006. (© Dylan Martinez/Reuters/Corbis)

commanded, managed and led his subordinates. This was to be done within a newly defined framework of 'police primacy' and he had regular operational meetings with his counterpart in the Royal Ulster Constabulary. As he pointed out, '[m]ajor decisions about how to prosecute counter-terrorism operations lay with the RUC; the Army played a supporting role'. Jackson left Northern Ireland around Easter 1992, shortly before the peace process got under way, triggered by the IRA ceasefire of 1994. General Jackson's experiences show us how military operations altered to meet the terrorist threat and they provide real insight into the commander's war in Northern Ireland.

The international dimension

Northern Ireland is a deeply divided society, and one which finds echoes around the world. Like rival Greek and Turkish Cypriots in the eastern Mediterranean or the Israelis and Palestinians in the Middle East, Protestant Unionists and Catholic nationalists share one land, but are separated by religion, history and culture. Reinforcing the conflict are the overlapping – albeit divergent – national identities held by both sides. Protestants regard themselves as British and wish to maintain the union with Great Britain, while Catholics wish to jettison these ties, abolish partition and unite Ireland. The strong bond between local communities and neighbouring states is common throughout Europe and the rest of the world, and it is echoed in much of the wall art decorating urban areas across Northern Ireland. In many ways one of the most telling aspects of the Troubles is the empathy the main parties to the conflict have with those undergoing similar trials and tribulations elsewhere.

The international dimension has been a constant feature of the Troubles ever since they exploded onto the streets in the late 1960s. Indeed, for the outside world the clashes between police, demonstrators and counter-demonstrators remained the conflict's defining images. Scenes of widespread disorder, police baton charges, masked gunmen and rioters, homes reduced to rubble, and streets awash with water-cannon spray and littered with smashed glass and bricks became commonplace.

Other conflicts around the world helped to fire up the imagination of many student radicals and civil rights activists. Interestingly, the Troubles erupted at a time when feelings in Northern Ireland were already running high, inflamed by global issues such as segregation in the American Deep South and the United States' intervention in Vietnam. In the US, armed militias like the Black Panthers took advantage of the civil disorder and could frequently be seen flanking those calling for the withdrawal of troops from south-east Asia, as well as those marching in solidarity with the North Vietnamese-sponsored insurgent groups. Ironically, some civil rights activists in Northern Ireland took to the streets to protest about these international problems more than about grievances closer to home. Unionists and nationalists would not remain insulated from the gathering storm of global protest for long.

Importantly, many IRA members saw their struggle in the context of worldwide national liberation struggles. Indeed, one former Provisional IRA volunteer admitted that at one time the organization had an 'embassy' in Algiers and had working contacts with the Popular Movement for the Liberation of Angola – Party of Labour (MPLA) and Zimbabwe African National Union – Patriotic Front (ZANU-PF). These links provided the IRA with much-needed logistical and financial support, as well as higher profile contacts with Colonel Gaddafi's Libyan regime and the African National Congress in South Africa. In an interview with the author the same IRA volunteer said:

[I]n reality I mean the contexts were good… Giving people solidarity who were fighting a post-colonial conflict… To me it consolidated my belief that we were an internationalist group. That they could relate to our struggle because we were socialist and secular, you know. It wasn't

Martin McGuinness stands in front of an anti-Thatcher mural on the Falls Road, 1985. (Hulton Archive/Getty Images)

just a nationalist push which inevitably, fatally, alas it turned out to be.

Loyalists tended to look closer to home, by seeking support for their cause in the Protestant heartlands of Glasgow and Merseyside. Scottish historian Ian S. Wood has chronicled how this support has manifested itself in what he calls '90 minute Loyalists', a term used to denote Northern Ireland soccer fans who regularly attend Glasgow Rangers football matches. Republicans have relied on supporters in Catholic parts of mainland Britain too, of course, many of whom gave the IRA financial support when they exported their armed struggle to England in the 1970s, 1980s and 1990s.

Soldiers from 1st Battalion, The Scots Guards, join with RUC officers in observing a three-minute silence to remember those killed in the September 11 attacks on the United States. The atrocities turned many Republican sympathizers in the US against terrorism, thus precipitating the end of the IRA's terror campaign. (IWM HU 98350)

Exporting the struggle

The threat posed by Irish Republican terrorists was a long-standing one and dated back to Irish Republican bomb attacks in London in the late 19th century. In December 1867, in an attempt to free one of their incarcerated members, the secretive Fenian Brotherhood carried out a bomb attack on Clerkenwell Prison, London. The lavish use of dynamite meant that the Fenians demolished a row of houses nearby, killing 12 people and injuring over 50. As the celebrated Communist thinker Karl Marx observed at the time:

The London masses, who have shown great sympathy towards Ireland, will be made wild and driven into the arms of a reactionary government. One cannot expect the London proletarians to allow themselves to be blown up in honour of Fenian emissaries.

Nevertheless, bombs in England became the powerful signature piece of each new incarnation of militant Irish Republicanism

over the next century. The threat of bombing would remain a thorn in the side of successive British governments, who were more susceptible to public calls for a solution to the 'Irish problem' to be found.

As a means of putting further pressure on the British state, the IRA took its war abroad, to military garrisons in Germany, the Netherlands and Gibraltar. In 1987 the IRA shot and killed an RAF serviceman in Roermond, near the German–Dutch border. Half an hour later the IRA blew up a car outside a nightclub in the village of Nieuwbergen, killing two RAF servicemen. In a statement released to the BBC, the IRA said '[w]e have a simple statement for Mrs Thatcher: Disengage from Ireland and there will be peace. If not, there will be no haven for your military personnel, and you will regularly be at airports awaiting your dead.' The IRA had now opened up a new front in their campaign of terror.

This wall mural in Hawthorn Street, West Belfast, depicts three IRA volunteers shot dead by the SAS in Gibraltar. The IRA took its 'armed struggle' abroad, targeting several British military bases in Germany and Gibraltar. (Aaron Edwards)

In perhaps one of the most controversial episodes in the Troubles, three IRA volunteers were killed by the SAS in Gibraltar on 6 March 1988. Although they had been unarmed at the time they were shot, intelligence suggested that the IRA suspects were preparing a car bomb aimed at British military personnel taking part in a parade. It had striking similarities with the Hyde Park outrage a number of years earlier. The 'Gibraltar Three', as they were later known, became martyrs for the Republican cause, and their deaths led to an outpouring of sympathy for the IRA not only from within Republican communities in Northern Ireland, but in Irish diaspora communities abroad.

RUC officers come under attack in Belfast after the signing of the Anglo-Irish Agreement. Unionists were hostile to the accord because it was brokered between London and Dublin without their consent. (Fred Hoare)

The search for peace

Nationalists and Republicans have always found sympathy and support in the many Irish diaspora communities scattered around the world, from the United States to Australia. The US connection, in particular, has borne both lucrative financial and moral support, as well as a steady flow of weapons. Throughout the Troubles, the British government was at pains to exert political pressure on those in the US who were offering their sympathies and support to violent Republicanism. In a speech to Irish-American corporate businessmen in 1977, the Northern Ireland Secretary of State Roy Mason challenged his audience to reconsider their support for militant Republicanism. 'It is through machinery, not machine guns; through business not bombs that the people of this great nation can assist the tiny but very deserving area of Northern Ireland to continue along the road to normality and prosperity,' he said.

That the IRA could command support from Irish diaspora communities abroad allowed those who were arguing for an end to hostilities in the early 1990s to situate their 'armed struggle' within the broader international environment. Such thinking was advanced by the IRA in its so-called Tactical Use of Armed Struggle (TUAS) document in the mid-1990s. Placing the Irish Republican struggle in a broader context allowed Gerry Adams and those dedicated to the Sinn Féin 'peace strategy' to forge ahead on the political front.

The transition from war to peace in the wake of the 1994 paramilitary ceasefires was by no means a smooth one. Under John Major the British government was insistent on decommissioning prior to entering any form of talks about the future of Northern Ireland. They had appointed US Senator George Mitchell as chairman of the international body on arms decommissioning, which was an integral component of the British and Irish governments' 'twin-track' process to address this outstanding issue. Mitchell was later asked to stay on to chair the all-party talks that had evolved out of the bilateral negotiations between the political parties and both governments. Although the IRA was not formally part of the negotiations that led up to the Belfast Agreement of 10 April 1998, it was represented by Sinn Féin.

Addressing members of the Provisional IRA in 2005, Adams said that he had always 'defended the right of the IRA to engage in armed struggle,' doing so on the basis that 'there was no alternative for those who would not bend the knee, or turn a blind eye to oppression, or for those who wanted a national republic'. However, with the onset of the peace process, he emphasized to them that there was now an 'alternative'. In his mind, the alternative was 'by building political support for Republican and democratic objectives across Ireland and by winning support for these goals internationally'. Adams successfully convinced the IRA of the need to create the conditions upon which a peace deal could be made. Within days of his speech the organization had called a halt to its armed campaign, and by September 2005 had decommissioned the last of its weapons.

In the Northern Ireland peace process, a range of international initiatives was tried; some had success, others failed completely.

The use of third-party mediators was tried in the 1970s, 1980s and 1990s. However, in the early days of the Troubles it was thought that Britain could fulfil this role. The British government wished to keep Northern Ireland off the international agenda and used its influence on the UN Security Council to do just that. However, as the descent into chaos continued in the wake of the imposition of direct rule in 1972, this was no longer thought possible. With the signing of the Sunningdale Agreement in 1973 and the Anglo-Irish Agreement in 1985 the British state warmed to the idea of greater intergovernmental co-operation with the Republic of Ireland, particularly in the realm of border security. Although Unionists rejected the Anglo-Irish Agreement, they begrudgingly accepted a more prominent role for the Dublin government by the time of the Good Friday Agreement in 1998, once constitutional safeguards had been put in place and enshrined by international law.

Northern Ireland was by no means unique in witnessing a clash between protestors and security forces in the late 1960s, as large-scale demonstrations were common in most European cities including London and Paris. What made the Troubles in Ulster unique, however, was the way in which the violence was portrayed as indelibly ethnic or tribal, and somewhat out of sync with the wider Cold War political confrontation between West and East. This caricature of Northern Ireland being 'a place apart' has since been challenged, particularly as ethnic-identity disputes exploded after the end of the Cold War in 1991.

A reporter's-eye-view: Malachi O'Doherty

For many ordinary people the Troubles were an unwelcome intrusion into their everyday lives. Ordinary lives were lived against the background noise of gunfire, bombings, rioting and the ever-present logic of sectarianism. Neighbour turned on neighbour and soon sectarianism, and the palpable fear of injury and death if one ventured into the 'wrong area', held Northern Ireland in a vice-like grip; this legacy of violence continues to divide local communities today.

The arrival of troops in 1969 was initially greeted with anxious optimism by Catholics, who felt that the British Army would protect them against a hostile Unionist regime and a predominantly Protestant police force. Within a matter of months relations between the Army and the Catholic community had soured, and a tiny minority of Republican militants opposed to Unionist rule embarked on violence aimed at defending their co-religionists. Initially, Republican violence was unco-ordinated and in fact, during an IRA General Army Convention in Dublin in December 1969, the organization split over a decision by leftist members to form a national liberation front and to end parliamentary abstentionism. The Dublin-based members became known as the Official IRA; those dissidents who returned to Belfast formed the Provisional IRA.

Both wings were militarily active in the 1970s and were responsible for many gun and bomb attacks. The Officials, however, called a ceasefire in 1972 and issued the following statement:

The Official IRA has decided to suspend armed military actions. News of the IRA's decision has caused a tremendous impact on the political situation and is regarded by observers as being the possible move that may yet prevent a full outbreak of a sectarian civil war.

The Provisional IRA maintained a more bloody-minded stance, holding firm – especially in the early 1970s – to the belief that with one big push they could drive out the British forces from Northern Ireland. Yet despite the rush to arms among some sections of the Catholic community, for the vast majority of people life continued as normal as the tribal lines were drawn between the two traditions. Fear took hold and violence escalated.

One person who has written extensively about his life experiences amid these tumultuous events is the Belfast-based journalist Malachi O'Doherty, who comes from the Andersonstown area of West Belfast. Born in 1951, the youngest of three children, O'Doherty lived at the corner of Riverdale Park Drive and Riverdale Park South. In the early years of the Troubles Riverdale Park Housing Estate became a hotbed for the Provisional IRA's 'E Company', a unit made up principally of seven men who had escaped from the Maidstone Prison Ship on 17 January 1972. Known locally in Republican circles as the 'Magnificent Seven', these detainees 'jumped ship' and swam the icy-cold waters of Belfast Lough, returning to safe houses in the Riverdale Park area. In the early 1970s the street outside Malachi's home formed the very hub of the fighting. As he recalled in his book *The Telling Year: Belfast, 1972*, '[t]here were nights then when I didn't sleep for the intense gunfire in the streets'.

Like many people living through the beginning of the Troubles in the early 1970s, O'Doherty recalled how a 'dark heavy air' descended over the province. As a young journalist working for the *Sunday News* he covered everything from the story of a lost cat to fresh food shortages. Much of his time was spent on these more mundane stories.

At that time, '[t]he paper's policy was to find other things than the troubles to be alarmed about', Malachi later wrote. However, with the bombing of McGurk's Bar in North Belfast, a UVF attack that killed 15 people, and Bloody Sunday, the *Sunday News* could no longer remain insulated from the violence. Immediately the junior reporter was thrust into the thick of the action. As he remarked in relation to events in Derry/Londonderry, 'the biggest story in Europe was on my doorstep'.

Covering the Troubles provided a dilemma for O'Doherty. After the fatal shootings by 1 Para on Bloody Sunday he prepared an article covering the episode. However, as he soon found out in a conversation with his editor, the pen could be just as powerful as the sword in shaping people's perceptions about the conflict:

Malachi O'Doherty reads from his book *The Telling Year: Belfast, 1972.* (Courtesy of Malachi O'Doherty)

> *On the following Saturday night, I was writing a story. Sean had come in to make sure we stuck to the rules: 'No comment. No loaded language.'*
> *'Can I use the word "massacre"?'*
> *'No, you can't.'*
> *'But what is the dictionary definition of massacre?'*
> *'I don't fucking care.'*

O'Doherty's boss was not alone, as most editors in the province knew only too well the fine line to be walked in reporting violent events that were *sub judice*. In this case the British government had appointed a senior judicial figure, Lord Chief Justice Widgery, to investigate the events of that day.

Living in Belfast at the time was an experience awash with curiosity for the young, roving reporter, who thought it odd that his neighbour who lived just a few hundred yards up his street could have little experience of living in 'a total ... warzone'. As he recalled in conversations with the author:

> *He would have heard gunfire but he would have had no conception. That you can live very close but unless it was under your nose you wouldn't know it was happening. And I think it was. So there's that extraordinary element of Belfast.*

Despite the uneven experience of different individuals, the Troubles raging outside were nevertheless having a wide-ranging effect on local communities:

> *There was a sense of very great stress when they were active but also when the Army came to the area and ... the moral dilemma which was impossible for me to deal with... I could have directed the Army to the arms dumps. But I did not feel that if the Army came in [it would have done any good]. Having said that. There were a few shooting incidents. Patsy McVeigh was shot ... The Army raided the place. Very often you saw those big Saracens and they also proliferated the areas in what we called the duck squads where a vehicle would drop them off and they would crawl around before being picked up.*

And as O'Doherty later revealed in *The Telling Year*, events outside increasingly encroached upon his family home:

> *I went to the head of the stairs as the door clattered open. The soldier was huge. His face was blackened and he held his rifle by the stock. He was wrong for a living room. He reduced it to a public space. I was not afraid; I was numb.*

The first thing to do was step forward and own up, the way I would have done at school, since to let anyone else take a beating for this would be unforgivable. With one hand the soldier clenched my shirt neck, twisted it to choke me and lifted me off the floor. My mother, in her nightie, was shrieking at him.

O'Doherty soon found himself threatened on two fronts: on the one hand by the actions of the British Army and on the other by the IRA. Although he was himself abused by some soldiers who subjected him to a series of electric shocks, he ardently rejected the IRA's claim to be defenders of the Catholic community.

O'Doherty's experience is indicative of the moral dilemma facing many ordinary people who grew up in extraordinary circumstances. Should they report what they were seeing to the authorities, or should they remain loyal in their support for the paramilitaries? For O'Doherty this was an artificial choice and he instead chose to oppose violence in all its forms.

IRA members, in particular, were often enraged by what O'Doherty wrote about them and lamented that he should have more empathy for what they were going through. Yet, as he points out in his influential book *The Trouble with Guns*, 'I have heard this before. It tires me. It presumes that anyone who grew up around the IRA, or with the IRA around them, would learn to see things their way.' As he observed:

There was an obvious paradox for me in that it was usually apologists for the IRA rather than the IRA themselves who argued that they had no choice but to conduct themselves as they did. It became part of the common lore that these were

people who had suffered, been humiliated and angered, and who were striking back out of their hurt and rage at the British Army or RUC.

As self-styled principled 'revolutionaries' the Provisionals had no shortage of sympathizers, from Irish-Americans with deep pockets in Boston, New York and Philadelphia to the intellectual support afforded to them by academics attracted to their subversive message.

O'Doherty has since gone on record to argue that 'the IRA never had a chance of victory, and had to kill for decades before it could learn that'. He has been forthright in his opposition to violence throughout the Troubles. From the 1990s onwards he covered the Troubles for BBC Northern Ireland, including broadcasting on the programmes *Talkback* and *Hearts and Minds*. He has since switched his critique of the peace process to those who were now parading the world stage and offering their services as peacemakers. In an article in the *Guardian* newspaper, he summed up the 'great men' interpretation of the Northern Ireland conflict as follows:

A lot of people got big jobs by talking up their achievements in peacemaking in Northern Ireland. It is all baloney. Peace came to Northern Ireland because the truculent parties got the best that was available to them after taking decades to work out that they had been pursuing political fantasies, not because Blair or anyone else showered them with wisdom and grace or applied any particular genius to contriving a deal.

There is certainly much that is commendable in this caustic view of how peace came to Northern Ireland.

Ceasefire to endgame

The 19th-century theorist of warfare Carl von Clausewitz observed in his masterpiece *On War* that '[w]hen whole communities go to war – whole peoples, and especially civilised peoples – the reason always lies in some political situation, and the occasion is always due to some political object'. The Northern Ireland Troubles could not be defined as a war according to the strict criteria laid down by international law, or, indeed, in the conventional military sense, of uniformed armies facing each other on a carefully defined battlefield where the 'normal' rules of warfare govern chivalrous acts of mortal combat. Nevertheless – especially for those who fought in them – the Troubles were a 'long war' few thought would ever end. That the Troubles did eventually subside, however, is in itself intriguing and worthy of further examination.

On the afternoon of 31 August 1994, BBC Northern Ireland's security correspondent Brian Rowan was contacted by a source close to the Provisional IRA leadership. The source instructed Rowan to travel to a café in West Belfast where he would be met and given a statement from the IRA's ruling Army Council. When he got to his destination he received a piece of paper announcing that the organization was declaring a ceasefire. It read:

Recognising the potential of the current situation and in order to enhance the democratic process and underlying our definitive commitment to its success, the leadership of the IRA have decided that as of midnight, August 31, there will be a complete cessation of military operations. All our units have been instructed accordingly.

This was the beginning of the end for the Troubles. But at the time few people expected the IRA to genuinely end its 'armed struggle' and even fewer expected it to do so against the backdrop of what many perceived to be a 'military stalemate'.

However, there was a much longer gestation to the IRA ceasefire than is generally acknowledged. While researching his book, *The Secret History of the IRA*, the New York-based journalist Ed Moloney unearthed evidence that Gerry Adams had been talking to British government representatives from as early as 1984. This back channel persisted despite Prime Minister Margaret Thatcher's public vow never to talk to terrorists. As she made clear in one speech:

I will have nothing to do with any organisation that practises violence. I have never seen anyone from ANC or the PLO or the IRA and would not do so. Nor will we have any truck with any of the organisations; we never negotiate with hostage taking or anything like that.

However, British government representatives had been meeting with IRA/Sinn Féin representatives behind the scenes since the beginning of the Troubles. Publicly, though, new ground was broken in a series of meetings between Adams and the leader of the SDLP, John Hume, in 1989 and again in 1992. The 'Hume–Adams dialogue', as it became known, was a process aimed at healing rifts in the nationalist community and finding a united way out of the conflict. For Hume it also served to focus attention on the external relationship between the Provisionals and the British state.

While these channels were important, it was the under-publicized contacts between members of the Protestant and Catholic clergy and Loyalist and Republican community representatives that eventually

Prime Minister John Major with Taoiseach Albert Reynolds after the signing of the Downing Street Declaration on 15 December 1993; without Major's tireless work it is unlikely that his successor, Tony Blair, would have had the same success in the Northern Ireland peace process. (© Matthew Polak/Sygma/Corbis)

paved the way towards peace on the ground. A number of peace processes involving the Provisional IRA were now under way; one involved a priest based at the Clonard Monastery in Belfast, Alec Reid; a local businessman and go-between in Derry/Londonderry, Brendan Duddy; and representatives of the British government. Meanwhile, Loyalist paramilitaries had nominated Protestant community representatives as the conduits through which information was then relayed to Reid and the Provisionals. Loyalists also reached out to the British and Irish governments, asking the Revd Robin Eames, Anglican Archbishop of Armagh, to communicate directly with London, while the Irish-based trades union activist Chris Hudson spoke to Dublin. All these individual streams trickled into the

fast-flowing tide that eventually contributed to the de-escalation of the military conflict.

With the Republican ceasefire in place, the onus was now on Loyalist paramilitary groupings to respond. The leaderships of the UVF and the UDA held clandestine meetings to thrash out the details of a ceasefire deal. As the UVF leader revealed in an interview with the author, this was a straightforward process:

Every UVF unit was consulted. There was no real opposition in the ranks – some worries and some scepticism but no outright opposition. Many of the politically motivated UVF members did have worries [but] the message was clear, the UVF is a counter-terrorist outfit. If PIRA aggression stops then the UVF has no military role to play. The next stage would be a political one. The message to the UVF troops on the ground was that if the PIRA stops, we stop because the Union is safe, next stage is for our political representatives – this message was also sent to the Nationalist community. When the PIRA called its ceasefire it proved that the analysis of the UVF leadership had been correct – this helped to lend it credibility.

Although the terms of reference for the ceasefire were agreed in secret in Monkstown on the outskirts of North Belfast, the wording of the statement was typed in the back office of the Progressive Unionist Party's headquarters on the Shankill Road by 'Gusty' Spence, the veteran UVF commander. Spence later read out the ceasefire statement at a press conference called by the Combined Loyalist Military Command, an umbrella group bringing together the UVF/RHC and UDA/UFF. In it he expressed 'abject and true remorse' on behalf of Loyalist paramilitaries, something which went further than the IRA's statement in recognizing the suffering inflicted on all innocent victims.

Scenes of jubilation followed in the wake of both ceasefires, albeit tinged with a sense of nervous optimism. Ceasefires had been tried before, of course, in the mid-1970s, but had not held; this time, though, there was a sense that conditions were different. By now all paramilitary groups had a strong degree of cohesion, central control and discipline. As Malachi O'Doherty wrote in his insightful book on the IRA, *The Trouble with Guns*, '[a] ceasefire is a military operation. The

authority of military leaders is required to maintain it.' O'Doherty maintained that although it was difficult to come to terms with people in the Republican and Loyalist groupings who may have murdered hundreds of people, 'when they have taken the job of containing their own murderous followers, through the authority they have acquired over those people by leading them to murder, then our interests in them are reversed'. Chillingly, the ceasefires and ensuing peace process, however imperfect, depended on paramilitary enforcers to take action that kept the violent conflict from re-emerging on the same scale as before.

All terrorist organizations operating in Northern Ireland have been inextricably linked to political parties and it was these legitimate organs that assumed responsibility for

This photograph depicts the immediate aftermath of a Provisional IRA attack on HQNI, 7 October 1996. Two no-warning car bombs were detonated by the IRA in a secure area of the base. The attack killed Warrant Officer James Bradwell and injured over 20 civilian staff and military personnel. The IRA renewed its ceasefire in July 1997. (IWM HU 98371)

A Chinook helicopter carries away the top half of a sangar. Security Forces bases were dismantled after each of the IRA's acts of decommissioning. (IWM HU 98360)

negotiating with British state officials. As it had done since the Anglo-Irish Agreement, Dublin continued to play a supporting role; under Irish Taoiseach Albert Reynolds and British Prime Minister John Major the warming of inter-governmental relations established another key pillar in the peace process.

The ceasefires did not completely silence the guns. It soon became obvious that dissent was growing within paramilitary ranks about the moves toward peace. On the one hand there had been disquiet in Republican circles about Major's insistence on IRA decommissioning before Sinn Féin were admitted into the talks. On the other hand, Unionist trepidations about the inclusion of Sinn Féin in inter-party talks boiled over into outright hostility. Here the Unionists held a trump card in that their representation at Westminster became an important bargaining chip with Major's minority Conservative Government. Ulster Unionist Party leader James Molyneaux and Democratic Unionist Party leader the Revd Ian Paisley were diametrically opposed to talks between the British government and

Sinn Féin. In Parliamentary debates on the Downing Street Declaration, Major said that 'there must be the clearest possible public renunciation of violence and then a decontamination period' before Sinn Féin could be admitted into discussions.

The IRA's South Armagh Brigade had always held considerable sway within the wider movement and its adherence to central IRA authority proved crucial. When it faltered, as it did in February 1996, its objections precipitated the IRA's return to war. During this period the IRA took its war to Britain, detonating a series of bombs across London and also huge car bombs in London's Docklands and Manchester city centre, causing millions of pounds worth of damage.

However, the political context soon shifted when New Labour was elected to office in Britain, under Prime Minister Tony Blair. Over the years since 1979 the Labour Party had been extremely vocal in its policy of a united Ireland by consent. However, as Mo Mowlam and Jonathan Powell have admitted in their memoirs, under Blair there was a move to exclude the 'Brits out' pressure groups – such as the Troops Out Movement – from the mainstream of Labour Party politics. New Labour's inclusive approach to the peace process helped to create the conditions under which the IRA renewed its ceasefire in July 1997. Within a short space of time Sinn Féin had been re-admitted into all-party talks, which eventually led to the signing of the Belfast/Good Friday Agreement on 10 April 1998.

Apart from reassuring Unionists that their position within the union was safe until a majority of people in the province voted otherwise, New Labour's approach to security policy emphasized the benefits of normalization. Normalization essentially meant the return of the British Army to barracks, soldiers exchanging helmets for berets, and the removal from Northern Ireland's landscape of Security Forces bases and watchtowers.

Between 1999 and 2004, the Army withdrew from eight bases it shared with the police. The figure was further reduced from

The Holy Cross dispute lasted for several months and was symptomatic of the so-called 'armed peace' that developed between Protestants and Catholics after the 1998 Belfast Agreement. (IWM HU 98352)

ten to zero in the four years leading up to the end of Operation *Banner* on 31 July 2007. Similarly, between 1999 and 2004, ten observation and communications posts were closed and by July 2005 the number had been further reduced to ten; by 31 July 2007 there were no military surveillance posts. In the last 24 months of Operation *Banner* the total number of military installations fell from 24 sites to 13. The number of military helicopter flying hours also dropped dramatically. Comparing the period from August 2004 to January 2005 with the period from August 2006 to January 2007, the Independent Monitoring Commission reported a reduction of 62 per cent.

Nevertheless, the hastening of the normalization process was made more difficult by the rampant sectarianism stirred up by Unionists and nationalists at Orange Order parades in places like Drumcree, near Portadown, and Whiterock in North Belfast. Here the Army was called in to support the police, who still lacked expertise in public-order drills and skills.

Events moved quickly. In July 2005 the IRA finally announced an end to its armed campaign:

> *The leadership of Óglaigh na hÉireann has formally ordered an end to the armed campaign. This will take effect from 4pm this afternoon.*
> *All IRA units have been ordered to dump arms.*
> *All Volunteers have been instructed to assist the development of purely political and democratic programmes through exclusively peaceful means. Volunteers must not engage in any other activities whatsoever.*

Nevertheless, while the winding-down of the military dimension effectively took the gun out of Northern Irish politics, it did not bring an end to sectarianism or the underlying causes of the Troubles.

Conclusion and consequences

Armed conflicts are typically followed by an audit of their causes and consequences. Those directly affected by the violence may be in search of reasons why it was visited on them and keen to find out whether the legacy of the past can be addressed in a manner that prevents a reoccurrence. Often,the parties to an ethnic conflict – such as the groups and communities diametrically opposed to each other – look back at what happened through rose-tinted glasses. It is unsurprising, therefore, that debates over the past in Northern Ireland have become more audible as the sounds of gunfire and explosions fade into the background.

Drawing lessons from armed conflicts is fraught with many pitfalls. Not all of them have similar causes, continuities and consequences. While it is tempting to draw comparisons between the British Army's

Troops from the King's Regiment exit Girdwood Barracks, North Belfast, in Saxon armoured vehicles. The wire mesh round the sangar was a security measure designed to deflect rocket-propelled grenades. (IWM HU 98390)

involvement in Northern Ireland and how it has approached contemporary operations elsewhere, such as in Iraq and Afghanistan, one must be careful not to make too many bold assumptions. Reflecting on his involvement in bringing an end to the Troubles, former British Prime Minister Tony Blair said, 'I know this from the Middle East peace process now, that I'm engaged in intimately, that one of the things that gives them hope is the success of the Northern Ireland process. It's a big symbol of change and possibility right round the world.' While this may be true, it is also indicative of the flawed belief that all conflicts can be resolved using the same formula.

Military lessons learned

Reflecting back over his 50-year career as a soldier, Field Marshal Bernard Montgomery concluded in his memoirs that '[w]e cannot see into the future accurately. But we can at least ensure that we do not disregard the lessons of the past: only a madman would do that.' As an institution the British Army actively sought to capture its own lessons from its deployment in Northern Ireland. These ranged from doctrine and training to the execution of major and minor operations. In the Army's official 'lessons learned' pamphlet, *Operation Banner: An Analysis of Military Operations in Northern Ireland*, there is a suggestion that the campaign was – on balance – a success, but that several key points ought to be noted for future operations.

The first is that there was no overall campaign authority for Operation *Banner*. Here the pamphlet argued that the decision-making process was chaotic at times and resulted in – among other things – the

intelligence agencies working to different agendas. This is a valid point made by authors such as Desmond Hamill and Mark Urban. Nevertheless, it is no coincidence that the Provisional IRA re-organized for its 'long war' strategy in the late 1970s, adopting a cellular unit structure, just as the increase in Britain's covert operations gathered momentum. It could be argued, however, that British military operations in Iraq between 2003 and 2009 also lacked such an overarching campaign authority. Furthermore, it is difficult to see how it could have been otherwise, when the Army played only a supporting role in Northern Ireland.

At a tactical level the Army learned a huge amount from Operation *Banner*. Respected journalist Patrick Bishop drew parallels with Afghanistan, concluding how '[t]here are some similarities. The skills and drills honed on the terraced streets of Belfast and Londonderry and the fields of Fermanagh and Tyrone have proved surprisingly useful in the river valleys of Helmand.' The Army's

First Minister Ian Paisley and Deputy First Minister Martin McGuinness entertain Taoiseach Bertie Ahern, Prime Minister Tony Blair and Secretary of State for Northern Ireland Peter Hain on 8 May 2007. (© Paul Faith/Pool/epa/Corbis)

training regime was second to none in preparing troops for deployment in-theatre, taking soldiers through tutorials on the IRA's arsenal of weapons, its bomb-making techniques, as well as its use of shoot-and-scoot tactics and armed propaganda (the use of violence to influence the wider political context). All this corporate knowledge came at a price, however, as it was built up from the direct exposure to terrorist violence.

As Carl von Clausewitz observed in *On War*, '[w]ar is the realm of physical exertion and suffering. These will destroy us unless we can make ourselves indifferent to them, and for this birth or training must provide us with a certain strength of body and soul.' In the abnormal environment of Northern Ireland soldiers conditioned themselves to adapt and survive under unimaginable stress, and mitigate the often-imminent threat to their lives. In Operation *Banner*, the Security Forces fought a 'battle of wills' against Republican and Loyalist terrorist groupings, holding the line while political initiatives attempted to forge a lasting peace in Northern Ireland.

Perhaps the biggest single stimulant in the Army's lesson-learning process was the decision by senior military commanders to take steps to avoid repeating mistakes. This willingness to admit its mistakes – while actively taking steps to ensure they are not repeated – is a prime example of the Army's professional ability to learn and adapt in highly pressurized environments. Reflecting on the release of the Saville Inquiry[4] report into 'Bloody Sunday', the Chief of the General Staff (subsequently Chief of the Defence Staff) Sir David Richards, said:

We must never forget the tragic events of Bloody Sunday. In the 38 years since that tragic day's events, lessons have been learned. The way the Army is trained, the way it works and the way it operates have all changed significantly.

Joining General Richards in his comments, his predecessor General Sir Mike Jackson, himself a veteran of the Troubles, said:

I recall that nearly 40 years ago in Northern Ireland the situation was grim with significant loss of life on all sides – not least by the Army. Over the 38 years of the Army's operational deployment in the province the vast majority of the some 250,000 soldiers who served there behaved admirably, often in the face of severe

provocation, and with the loss of several hundred lives and 6,000 wounded. Northern Ireland today is now a very different place, not least because of those sacrifices and I ask that Lord Saville's report be seen in this context.

The Army had indeed learnt valuable lessons in Northern Ireland, just as it has done in all of its operational theatres since 1945.

Notwithstanding these candid admissions, there has also been a tendency to learn the wrong lessons from Operation *Banner*. The Army's official pamphlet on military operations in Northern Ireland said for instance that the 'few bombs that were placed in Service married quarters areas appear to have been placed to tie down troops, rather than to kill or maim. The reasons probably lie in the self-image of the IRA as an Army with its own sense of morality, honour and justice.' While on the face of it such monochrome remembrances of the Troubles are harmless, they serve to seriously underplay the ruthlessness of terrorist groups like the IRA. Moreover, by playing up the political 'nobility' of the Republican campaign this account obscures the brutal reality of IRA violence and constructs misleading interpretations out of bad history.

Rather than consciously avoid casualties among its opponents, the IRA deliberately targeted Security Forces personnel and the civilians working for them. In 1972 the Official IRA carried out a no-warning bombing of 2 Para's mess in Aldershot Army Garrison, Hampshire, killing six civilian workers and a Roman Catholic padre. In the late 1980s the IRA attempted to mortar the families' quarters in a UDR barracks at Steeple in Antrim. And in perhaps the most brazen attempt to kill and maim Security Forces personnel, the IRA detonated two huge car bombs in Thiepval Barracks, Lisburn, killing one soldier and injuring over 20 civilian and military personnel, on 7 October 1997. In undertaking these operations and countless others, the IRA earned a reputation as one of the most ruthless terrorist organizations in history.

---

4   Lord Saville was chosen by the New Labour government to head up the 'Bloody Sunday' Inquiry in 1998. A former High Court Judge, he was appointed a Law Lord in 1997 and went on to become Justice of the Supreme Court of the United Kingdom between 2009 and 2010. He was hand-picked because he was considered to be 'less stuffy' and more of 'a modernizing judge', who could navigate a route through the choppy waters of this emotionally intense episode in Northern Ireland's past.

Political lessons learned

Like the Army, the British government also learned lessons from its long involvement in Northern Ireland. In a speech to the Mid-Atlantic Club in Washington, DC, on 17 October 1977 the then-Northern Ireland Secretary of State, Roy Mason, said: 'Perhaps one of the most important lessons learned in Northern Ireland over the past few years – and it is a lesson which has important international implications – is that in a democratic society there is no way forward through the use of violence.'

This was a recurrent theme in the government's official language throughout the Troubles. It dovetailed with security policy in implying that there could be no military solution to the conflict. Thus, the main task of the police and Army was to stabilize the security situation while various political initiatives were attempted, from the Sunningdale Agreement in 1973 through to the Good Friday Agreement in 1998. The

Old enemies agree a timetable for power-sharing. Ian Paisley and Gerry Adams – as leaders of the two largest parties – finally agree to form a power-sharing executive. Seated next to Paisley is his deputy Peter Robinson, who succeeded him when he stepped down in 2008. (© Pool/Reuters/Corbis)

political context was vitally important as it permitted the British government to enter into negotiations with the Provisional IRA at opportune moments in the 1970s, 1980s and 1990s. In the words of journalist Malachi O'Doherty:

Another lesson for militants and state security forces: don't kill anybody unless you really have to. Especially, do not kill the leaders of the militant groups. If you want leaders to be able to control the whole movement underneath them, then you have to leave them in place for long enough to secure credibility and influence. Don't fragment an enemy you ultimately hope to negotiate with.

The willingness of states to 'talk to terrorists' has become more evident since the

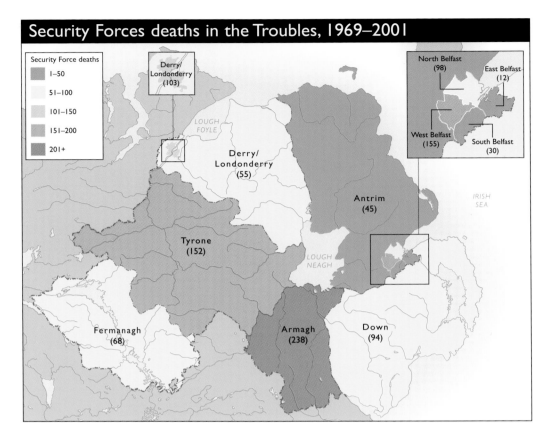

Security Forces deaths in the Troubles, 1969–2001

Security Force deaths
- 1–50
- 51–100
- 101–150
- 151–200
- 201+

North Belfast (98)
East Belfast (12)
West Belfast (155)
South Belfast (30)

Derry/Londonderry (103)

LOUGH FOYLE

Derry/Londonderry (55)

Antrim (45)

IRISH SEA

Tyrone (152)

LOUGH NEAGH

Fermanagh (68)

Armagh (238)

Down (94)

bedding-down of the peace process in the late 1990s. The merits of dialogue between representatives of the various terrorist groups and the British and Irish governments have been recognized and applauded on the world stage. However, it is often forgotten how political space was created only in the wake of an application of coercion, mainly on the part of the British government and its Security Forces, both to cajole and entice these groups into suing for peace.

From the late 1970s the British government returned to the first principle that in combating terrorism and insurgency, the lead must always be taken by the civilian authority. A number of directives were issued through the Northern Ireland Office and a new plan, *The Way Ahead*, placed the RUC at the forefront of the counter-terrorist fight. Police–Army co-operation at the operational and tactical levels had become a success story by the mid-1990s.

The human cost

Without question, the single biggest group affected by the Troubles was the local civilian population. Comparing conflict-related deaths is a macabre business. The number of deaths in Northern Ireland might seem small compared with the total population, but scaled proportionately, had the conflict taken place in Great Britain, it would have claimed 100,000 lives, or 500,000 in the United States.

The detailed analysis of Security Forces deaths is equally revealing. Estimates for the number of service personnel killed in action during Operation *Banner* vary. In 2007 the former Chief of the Defence Staff, Sir Jock Stirrup, put the figure at 651 and 6,307 wounded, while an official MoD tally from 2008 records a total of 763 (and 6,116 wounded), a figure which includes 651 Army and Royal Marines personnel,

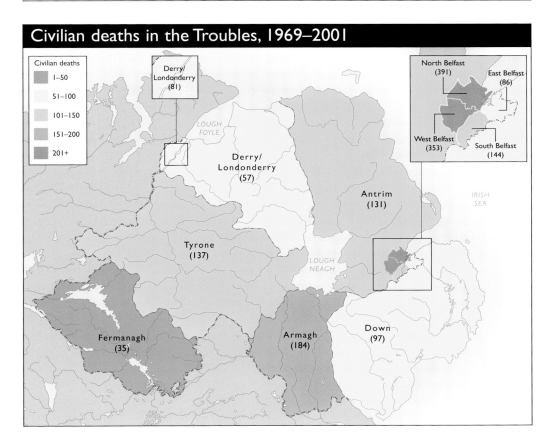

Civilian deaths in the Troubles, 1969–2001

Civilian deaths
- 1–50
- 51–100
- 101–150
- 151–200
- 201+

Derry/Londonderry (81)

North Belfast (391)
East Belfast (86)
West Belfast (353)
South Belfast (144)

LOUGH FOYLE

Derry/Londonderry (57)

Antrim (131)

IRISH SEA

Tyrone (137)

LOUGH NEAGH

Fermanagh (35)

Armagh (184)

Down (97)

one Royal Navy serviceman, 50 members of the UDR/Royal Irish Regiment, ten members of the Territorial Army, and 51 military personnel murdered outside Northern Ireland. These figures are, however, somewhat misleading. The more reliable CAIN/Malcolm Sutton database puts the number of fatalities much higher. Between 1969 and 1997, it records the deaths of 502 British Army and Royal Marines personnel, 203 members of the UDR/RIR, seven Territorial Army members and 58 military personnel murdered outside Northern Ireland, giving a total of 770 military personnel killed. In contrast, the RUC lost 301 officers. However, these statistics mask the oft-forgotten truth that 40 former members of the UDR and 18 former members of the RUC died at the hands of Republican terrorists, for the IRA did not distinguish between on-duty, off-duty and former members. Other MoD

statistics show that the UDR/RIR suffered 274 dead between 1971 and 2002, disproportionately higher than any other British Army regiment.

In comparable terms one could argue that Operation *Banner* was just as intense as Operation *Telic*, the British intervention in Iraq. Of the 179 British service personnel killed in Iraq between 2003 and 2009, 113 died in hostilities; the remainder included seven killed in 'friendly fire' incidents, 45 in accidents, two by suicide, and 12 in other circumstances. In sharp contrast to Operation *Telic*, Britain's involvement in Afghanistan has been much bloodier. While only five soldiers died between 2001 and 2005, a total of 300 personnel have been killed in hostilities since 2006. A further 35 have died from disease, non-combat injuries or accidents. To date (writing in March 2011), 2009 was the bloodiest year for British forces in

Secretary of State for Northern Ireland Dr Mo Mowlam visits soldiers during operations at Drumcree on 10 July 1998. (IWM HU 98386)

Afghanistan, with 108 military personnel killed in action. It is worth keeping this in mind because in the four years after 1971, when the IRA went on the offensive against British troops, approximately 318 soldiers were killed by hostile action.

Over the course of Operation *Banner* the number of Security Forces members and civilians killed averaged about one to two every day for the 25-year period between 1969 and 1997. The bloodiest year of the Troubles was 1972, when 497 people died, including 130 British soldiers. The most dangerous areas for Security Forces personnel throughout the Troubles were County Armagh, West Belfast and County Tyrone. One 'taboo' subject often overlooked by books on Operation *Banner* is the high number of deaths indirectly related to the Troubles; from road traffic accidents to suicides brought about by post-traumatic stress disorder. Although it is difficult to

estimate how many soldiers have taken their own lives, the Police Federation for Northern Ireland has said that up to 70 RUC/PSNI officers have committed suicide, many with their personal-issue service revolver. In his excellent oral history research on the Army in Northern Ireland, Ken Wharton assembled a complete Roll of Honour, which – incredibly – records over 1,300 military deaths.

The human cost of violence is poorly reflected in the journalistic and academic literature on the Troubles. Because of the political core of the Republican and Loyalist terrorist campaigns, there has been a tendency to glorify the 'noble dead' and revise history to suit present-day political agendas. Poets, on the other hand, have been more forthright in their stark warnings of the futility of sectarian conflict. In his poem 'Wounds', Michael Longley gives us an insight into how the Troubles permeated every aspect of everyday life:

Also a bus-conductor's uniform –
He collapsed beside his carpet-slippers
Without a murmur, shot through the head

By a shivering boy who wandered in
Before they could turn the television down
Or tidy away the supper dishes.
To the children, to a bewildered wife,
I think 'Sorry Missus' was what he said.

Despite the optimism unleashed by the 1994 ceasefires and the Good Friday Agreement almost four years later, the Troubles served to strengthen the deep ethnic, national and religious fault-lines. And while the paramilitary ceasefires may have triggered a winding-down of the military campaigns, the sectarianism that animated these struggles has not lessened. The Troubles have left behind a terrible legacy, of dead and wounded on all sides, scarring people it affected both directly and indirectly, not only in Northern Ireland, but also across the British Isles, in a way that may take generations to heal. At one time many people thought the conflict was simply insoluble. Nevertheless, the transformation from long war to long peace has marked a step-change in relationships between Protestant Unionist and Catholic nationalist communities. The history of Operation *Banner* offers us the opportunity to understand the past and to draw lessons from what really happened, so that similar tragedies can be avoided in the future.

Bibliography

Primary sources

Archives
The National Archives of the United Kingdom (Kew, London):
CAB/129/144, 'Press notice following meeting between Home Secretary James Callaghan and influential Roman Catholic deputation from Belfast', dated 12 September 1969
CAB/128/48, 'Top Secret Meeting of the Cabinet', dated 27 July 1972
CJ 3/13, 'Relations with the Government of Northern Ireland: Formal Requests for Military Assistance and Subsequent Role of the Military', all documents dated August 1969
DEFE 70/214, Appended Letter to the document 'The Future of Internment', dated 14 February 1972
DEFE 70/644, 'IRA Mine Warfare – Command Detonated Mines', dated 7 August 1972
DEFE 24/1945, 'Armed Helicopters in Northern Ireland', dated 20 March 1973
DEFE 24/1226, 'Northern Ireland: Notes of Meetings', all documents dated 1976 and 1977
DEFE 24/1618, 'Working Group on Security Forces Capability', all documents dated 1977
DEFE 11/918, 'Possible Loyalist Disturbances in Northern Ireland', memos dated 26 and 27 April and 2 and 4 May 1977
DEFE 11/918, 'PM's Private Secretary to Northern Ireland Office', dated 28 April 1977
DEFE 11/918, 'Correspondence from Roy Mason to Fred Malley', dated 18 May 1977
DEFE 11/918, 'Directive for the General Officer Commanding Northern Ireland as Director of Military Operations', dated 28 July 1977
DEFE 11/918, 'Transcript of a Speech by Roy Mason to the Mid-Atlantic Club,

Washington D.C.', dated 17 October 1977
DEFE 11/918, 'Commander Land Forces Operational Summary for the 2 Weeks ending 19 October 1977', dated 19 October 1977
FCO 87/221, 'Report by Frank Steele of a Visit to the Bogside and Creggan on 4 and 5 April 1973', dated 5 April 1973
PREM 15/1009, 'Top Secret: Notes of a Meeting with Representatives of the Provisional IRA', dated 21 June 1972
PREM 15/1011, 'Top Secret – Perimeter – Northern Ireland: Draft Rules of Engagement', dated 26 July 1972
Unknown reference, 'Report entitled 'Subversion in the UDR' prepared by British Military Intelligence in August 1973', dated August 1973. Available at: <http://cain.ulst.ac.uk/publicrecords/1973/subversion_in_the_udr.htm> (accessed 17 September 2010)

London School of Economics and Political Science Archives:
Papers of Merlyn Rees (Baron Merlyn-Rees), 1920–2006

Public Records Office of Northern Ireland (Belfast):
GOV 3/17/3, Correspondence between Lieutenant-General Sir Harry Tuzo and the Governor of Northern Ireland, Lord Grey of Naunton, relating to the security situation in border areas, dated 4 and 7 September 1971
PRONI, PM 5/2/1, Private letter from Dr Norman Laird, Stormont MP for St Anne's, to Major James Chichester-Clark, 27 September 1969

Special Collections, Bodleian Library:
Clement Attlee, Harold Wilson and James Callaghan Papers

Interviews

Interview with the leader of the UVF,
9 September 2004. This individual has
allegedly commanded the organization
since the 1970s

Interview with Billy Mitchell, 16 September
2005. Former high-ranking member of the
UVF in the 1970s and Progressive
Unionist Party strategist from the early
1990s until his death in 2006

Interview with a former British Army staff
officer, 21 June 2010. A former major who
manned the Army's 'press desk' at HQNI,
1970–73

Interview with Tommy Gorman, 23 June
2010. Former member of the Provisional
IRA and senior operations officer in the
Belfast Brigade's engineering department

Interview with Jon McCourt, 23 June 2010.
Former member of the Derry IRA,
1969–75; now well-respected peace
advocate in Derry City

Interview with a former member of 2 Para,
and later the UDR/RIR, 31 August 2010.
Served several tours throughout Northern
Ireland in the 1970s, 1980s and 1990s

Interview with a former member of the UDR,
1 September 2010. Based in the County
Derry/Londonderry area and who served
from 1971 until 1992 in both a part-time
and full-time capacity

Interview with a former Royal Engineers
Search Adviser, 17 September 2010. Served
several tours in the 1970s and 1980s

Interview with a former officer from the
UDR/RIR, 22 September 2010. Based
mainly in the County Antrim area

Official publications

Cameron, *Disturbances in Northern Ireland*,
Presented to Parliament September 1969,
Cmd. 532 (Belfast, 1969)

Independent Monitoring Commission,
Reports of the IMC, 2004–2010. Accessed at:
<http://www.independentmonitoring
commission.org> (accessed 13 October 2010)

Northern Ireland Community Relations
Commission Research Unit, *Flight:
A Report on Population Movement in Belfast
during August 1971* (Belfast, 1971)

Northern Ireland House of Commons,
Parliamentary Debates: Official Report
(Hansard), 1921–72

Northern Ireland Office, *The Agreement,
1998*. Archived at:
<http://www.nio.gov.uk/agreement.pdf>
(accessed 15 July 2010)

Saville, *Report of the Bloody Sunday Inquiry*,
Archived at: <http://report.bloody-sunday-
inquiry.org> (accessed 15 June 2010)

Scarman, *Violence and Civil Disturbances in
Northern Ireland in 1969*. Presented to
Parliament April 1972, Cmd. 566
(Belfast, 1972)

Secondary sources

Articles and book chapters

Benest, David, 'Aden to Northern Ireland,
1966–76' in Strachan, Hew, ed., *Big Wars
and Small Wars: The British Army and the
Lessons of War in the Twentieth Century*,
London, 2006, pp. 115–44

Bennett, Huw, 'From Direct Rule to
Motorman: Adjusting British Military
Strategy for Northern Ireland in 1972',
Studies in Conflict and Terrorism, 33(6)
(June 2010), pp. 511–32

Dixon, Paul, 'Hearts and Minds? British
Counter-insurgency in Northern Ireland',
Journal of Strategic Studies, 32(3)
(June 2009), pp. 445–74

Edwards, Aaron, 'Social Democracy and
Partition: The British Labour Party and
Northern Ireland, 1951–64', *Journal of
Contemporary History*, 42(4) (October
2007), pp. 595–612

Edwards, Aaron, 'Drawing a Line under
the Past', *Peace Review: A Journal of Social
Justice*, 20(2) (April–June 2008),
pp. 209–17

Edwards, Aaron, '"Unionist Derry is Ulster's
Panama": The Northern Ireland Labour
Party and the Civil Rights Issue', *Irish
Political Studies*, 23(3) (September 2008),
pp. 363–85

Edwards, Aaron, 'Abandoning Armed
Struggle? The Ulster Volunteer Force as
a Case-study of Strategic Terrorism in

Northern Ireland', *Studies in Conflict and Terrorism*, 32(2) (February 2009), pp. 146–66

Edwards, Aaron, 'Misapplying Lessons Learned? Analysing the Utility of British Counter-insurgency Strategy in Northern Ireland, 1971–76', *Small Wars and Insurgencies*, 21(2) (June 2010), pp. 303–30

Edwards, Aaron, 'Interpreting New Labour's Political Discourse on the Peace Process' in Hayward, Katy, and Catherine O'Donnell, eds *Political Discourse and Conflict Resolution: Debating Peace in Northern Ireland*, Abingdon, 2010, pp. 41–67

Grayson, Richard S., 'The Place of the First World War in Contemporary Irish Republicanism in Northern Ireland', *Irish Political Studies*, 25(3) (September 2010), pp. 325–45

Iron, Colonel Richard, 'Britain's Longest War: Northern Ireland, 1967–2007' in Marston, Daniel and Malkasian, Carter, eds, *Counterinsurgency in Modern Warfare*, Oxford, 2009, pp. 167–84

Irwin, Sir Alistair, and Mahoney, Mike, 'The Military Response' in Dingley, James, ed., *Combating Terrorism in Northern Ireland*, London, 2009, pp. 198–226

Kirk-Smith, Michael, and Dingley, James, 'Countering Terrorism in Northern Ireland: The Role of Intelligence', *Small Wars and Insurgencies*, 20(3–4) (September–December 2009), pp. 551–73

Neumann, Peter R., 'Winning the "War on Terror"? Roy Mason's Contribution to Counter-terrorism in Northern Ireland', *Small Wars and Insurgencies*, 14(3) (Autumn 2003), pp. 45–64

Newsinger, John, 'From Counter-insurgency to Internal Security: Northern Ireland, 1969–1992', *Small Wars and Insurgencies*, 6(1) (Spring 1995), pp. 88–111

O'Dochartaigh, Niall, 'Bloody Sunday: Error or Design?', *Contemporary British History*, 24(1) (March 2010), pp. 89–108

O'Doherty, Malachi, 'Lessons from Northern Ireland', *The Guardian*, 8 May 2007

O'Doherty, Malachi, 'Blair's Flaky Credentials', *The Guardian*, 26 June 2007

Books

Barthorp, Michael, *Crater to the Creggan: The History of the Royal Anglian Regiment, 1964–1974*, London, 1976

Bean, Kevin, *The New Politics of Sinn Féin*, Liverpool, 2007

Bew, Paul, Ireland: *The Politics of Enmity*, 1789-2006, Oxford, 2007

Bowyer Bell, J., *The IRA, 1968–2000: Analysis of a Secret Army*, London, 2000

Callaghan, James, *A House Divided: The Dilemma of Northern Ireland*, London, 1973

Clausewitz, Carl von. *On War*, edited and translated by Michael Howard and Peter Paret, Princeton, NJ, 1989

Collins, Eamon, *Killing Rage*, London, 1998

Dannatt, General Sir Richard, *Leading from the Front: The Autobiography*, London, 2010

Dewar, Lieutenant-Colonel Michael, *The British Army in Northern Ireland: Revised Edition*, London, 1985

Dillon, Martin, *The Dirty War*, London, 1991

Dillon, Martin, *The Shankill Butchers: A Case-study of Mass Murder*, London, 1991

Dillon, Martin, *Killer in Clowntown: Joe Doherty, the IRA and the Special Relationship*, London, 1992

Dillon, Martin, *Stone Cold: The True Story of Michael Stone and the Milltown Massacre*, London, 1993

Dixon, Paul, *Northern Ireland: The Politics of War and Peace* , Basingstoke, 2008

Edwards, Aaron, and Bloomer, Stephen, eds, *Transforming the Peace Process in Northern Ireland: From Terrorism to Democratic Politics*, Dublin, 2008

English, Richard, *Armed Struggle: The History of the IRA*, London, 2003

Evelegh, Robin, *Peacekeeping in a Democratic Society*, London, 1978

Geraghty, Tony, *The Irish War: The Military History of a Domestic Conflict*, London, 1998

Hamill, Desmond, *Pig in the Middle: The Army in Northern Ireland, 1969–1984*, London, 1985

Hanley, Brian, and Millar, Scott, *The Lost Revolution: The Story of the Official IRA and the Worker's Party*, Dublin, 2009

Harnden, Toby, *'Bandit Country': The IRA and South Armagh*, London, 2000

Hennessey, Thomas, *A History of Northern Ireland: 1921–1996*, Dublin, 1997

Hennessey, Thomas, *The Northern Ireland Peace Process: Ending the Troubles?*, Dublin, 2000

Hennessey, Thomas, *The Origins of the Troubles*, Dublin, 2005

Hennessey, Thomas, *The Evolution of the Troubles, 1970–72*, Dublin, 2007

Holland, Jack and Phoenix, Susan, *Phoenix: Policing the Shadows – The Secret War against Terrorism in Northern Ireland*, London, 1996

Jackson, General Sir Mike, *Soldier: The Autobiography*, London, 2007

Kitson, Frank, *Low Intensity Operations: Subversion, Insurgency, Peacekeeping*, London, 1971

Kitson, Frank, *Bunch of Five*, London, 1977

McDonald, Henry, and Cusack, John, *UVF: The Endgame*, Dublin, 2008

McGrattan, Cillian, *Northern Ireland, 1968–2008: The Politics of Retrenchment*, Basingstoke, 2010

McKittrick, David, Kelters, Seamus, Feeney, Brian, and Thorton, Chris, *Lost Lives: The Stories of the Men, Women and Children who Died as a Result of the Northern Ireland Troubles*, Edinburgh, 2001

Moloney, Ed, *A Secret History of the IRA*, London, 2003

Morton, Peter, *Emergency Tour: 3 Para in South Armagh*, Wellingborough, 1989

Murray, Raymond, *The SAS in Ireland*, Cork, 2004

Neumann, Peter R., *Britain's Long War: British Strategy in the Northern Ireland Conflict, 1969–98*, Basingstoke, 2003

O'Dochartaigh, Niall, *From Civil Rights to Armalites: Derry and the Birth of the Irish Troubles*, Cork, 1997

O'Doherty, Malachi, *The Trouble with Guns: Republican Strategy and the Provisional IRA*, Belfast, 1998

O'Doherty, Malachi, *The Telling Year: Belfast 1972*, Dublin, 2007

Oppenheimer, A. R., *IRA: The Bombs and the Bullets – A History of Deadly Ingenuity*, Dublin, 2009

Patterson, Henry, *Ireland since 1939: The Persistence of Conflict*, Dublin, 2006

Potter, John, *A Testimony to Courage: The Regimental History of the Ulster Defence Regiment*, Barnsley, 2001

Powell, Jonathan, *Great Hatred, Little Room: Making Peace in Northern Ireland*, London, 2008

Purdie, Bob, *Politics in the Streets: The Origins of the Civil Rights Movement in Northern Ireland*, Belfast, 1990

Rennie, James, *The Operators: Inside 14 Company – The Army's Top Secret Elite*, London, 1996

Ryder, Chris, *The Ulster Defence Regiment: An Instrument of Peace?*, London, 1991

Ryder, Chris, *A Special Kind of Courage: 321 EOD Squadron – Battling the Bombers*, London, 2005

Smith, M.L.R., *Fighting for Ireland? The Military Strategy of the Irish Republican Movement*, London, 1997

Taylor, Peter, *Provos: The IRA and Sinn Féin*, London, 1998

Taylor, Peter, *Loyalists*, London, 2000

Taylor, Peter, *Brits: The War against the IRA*, London, 2002

Urban, Mark, *Big Boys Rules: The SAS and the Struggle against the IRA*, London, 1992

Wood, Ian S., *Crimes of Loyalty: A History of the UDA*, Edinburgh, 2006

Websites

Britain's Small Wars: The History of British Military Conflicts since 1945, <http://www.britains-smallwars.com/> (accessed 10 September 2010)

Conflict Archive on the Internet (CAIN), <http://cain.ulst.ac.uk/index.html> (accessed 12 September 2010)

Free Derry Museum, <http://www.museumoffreederry.org/> (accessed 12 September 2010)

Operation *Banner* – British Armed Forces in Northern Ireland: The Troubles, <http://www.operationbanner.com/> (accessed 10 September 2010)

Audio-visual sources

British Universities Film and Video Council. Archived at <http://radio.bufvc.ac.uk/> (accessed 24 August 2010)

Index